PENGUIN
SPECIALS

Penguin Specials fill a gap. Written by some of today's
most exciting and insightful writers, they are short
enough to be read in a single sitting — when you're
stuck on a train; in your lunch hour; between dinner
and bedtime. Specials can provide a thought-provoking
opinion, a primer to bring you up to date, or a striking
piece of fiction. They are concise, original and affordable.

To browse digital and print Penguin Specials titles,
please refer to **www.penguin.com.au/penguinspecials**

The Rise and Fall of the House of Bo

JOHN GARNAUT

PENGUIN BOOKS

Published by the Penguin Group
Penguin Group (Australia)
707 Collins Street, Melbourne, Victoria 3008, Australia
(a division of Pearson Australia Group Pty Ltd)
Penguin Group (USA) Inc.
375 Hudson Street, New York, New York 10014, USA
Penguin Group (Canada)
90 Eglinton Avenue East, Suite 700, Toronto, Canada ON M4P 2Y3
(a division of Pearson Penguin Canada Inc.)
Penguin Books Ltd
80 Strand, London WC2R 0RL, England
Penguin Ireland
25 St Stephen's Green, Dublin 2, Ireland
(a division of Penguin Books Ltd)
Penguin Books India Pvt Ltd
11 Community Centre, Panchsheel Park, New Delhi – 110 017, India
Penguin Group (NZ)
67 Apollo Drive, Rosedale, North Shore 0632, New Zealand
(a division of Pearson New Zealand Ltd)
Penguin Books (South Africa) (Pty) Ltd
24 Sturdee Avenue, Rosebank, Johannesburg 2196, South Africa
Penguin (Beijing) Ltd
7F, Tower B, Jiaming Center, 27 East Third Ring Road North, Chaoyang
District, Beijing 100020, China
Penguin Books Ltd, Registered Offices: 80 Strand, London, WC2R 0RL,
England

First published by Penguin Group (Australia), 2012
This edition published by Penguin Group (Australia), 2013

Copyright © John Garnaut, 2012

The moral right of the author has been asserted

penguin.com.au

ISBN: 9780143569350

CONTENTS

The Rock Star of Chinese Politics................................. I

A Dynastic Succession 8

The Red Terror.. 19

The Prince of Dalian.. 34

The Chongqing Model.. 48

Spectre of the Cultural Revolution 65

Murder on the Yangtze 80

The Great Escape.. 103

The Fall of Bo, Xi's Rise.................................... 116

Acknowledgements.. 135

Notes 137

The Rock Star of Chinese Politics

In March of each year, the Chinese capital comes to a standstill for the ten-day gathering of the National People's Congress at the Soviet-designed Great Hall of the People. Traffic is blocked, vagrants are swept from the city, lawyers and intellectuals are sent away or detained and media censorship steps up an extra gear, while journalists from the Xinhua News Agency interview their foreign counterparts about this showcase of democracy. The fuss seems out of proportion for a legislature appointed by the Communist Party and which has never rejected a law bill put before it. In recent years there have been, however, two flickers of transparency and political showmanship that the Beijing press corps learned to look forward to. One was the closing press conference presided over by the leadership's lone advocate for democratic reforms,

Wen Jiabao, which was the only opportunity that journalists had to ask real questions of a top-ranked leader and to expect a meaningful reply. The other was the appearance of Wen's ideological adversary: the rock star of Chinese politics, Bo Xilai.

At the time of the 2012 Congress, Bo Xilai was a provincial leader who was not a member of the nine-member Politburo Standing Committee, and yet he seemed to be setting the national political agenda. Since being sent to run the Yangtze River metropolis of Chongqing in late 2007 he had draped himself in neo-Maoist iconography and led an orchestrated craze of 'red singing' of patriotic revolution-era songs across the nation. He had attracted unprecedented praise from several of his superiors – most notably from the incoming president, Xi Jinping – for a war he was waging against corruption, inequality and mafia-state collusion. He was seen as the custodian of the Party's revolutionary ideals, fighting to live up to Mao's instruction to 'serve the people', at a time when the Party and the country had lost its way. He had become the poster boy for socialism's true believers and a magnet for all who were attracted to the lure of rising power. Some who had grown up and risen through the ranks with Bo believed he wanted to ultimately eclipse Xi Jinping and become the most powerful man in China after the leadership transition of November 2012.

In previous years, Bo had been mobbed at the National People's Congress by the Hong Kong media. This year even local Chinese journalists swarmed to see him perform, although they would never be able to report a word, because they knew they would be watching history being made.

At this point, only a select few with high security clearances in China, the United States and close US allies were privy to the sordid allegations of bribery, brutality and murder that Bo's recently sacked police chief, Wang Lijun, had been levelling against the Bo family. But everybody knew the great red hope of Chinese politics was in trouble and that his enemies were circling. 'The climate in Chongqing is very different from the climate in Beijing,' He Guoqiang, the head of the Central Commission for Discipline Inspection, had warned Bo and his supporters in the Chongqing room of the Great Hall, only days before.[1] 'So I hope that everyone will take care against the cold and stay warm, and be careful to stay healthy.'

Bo kept the media waiting for the first week of the Congress, skipped an important public session, and then on 9 March appeared without the customary notice in the Chongqing room. He was clearly tired, looking pale with bags under his eyes, after late-night sessions rallying his colleagues and negotiating his fate. But there was no hiding the prodigious charisma and self-belief that had helped him to mobilise a large corner of the country, independent of central command, in a way that no other leader had done since 1949. Wearing a sharp navy suit and yellow tie, he sat with his back against a spectacular photo-backdrop of Chongqing's neon skyline, as if to remind the crowd of the phenomenon he had built, while camera flashes lit up the room.

A month earlier, Wang Lijun, Bo's former police chief and legendary right-hand man, had shown so little trust in both his patron and the Chinese justice system that he had fled into the arms of China's great rival, at the US Consulate in nearby Chengdu. Earlier that week, President Hu Jintao had revealed his view of both Wang and the Americans by telling delegates that Wang had 'betrayed the country and gone over to the enemy', according to a Chinese intelligence official. Journalists assembled at the Great Hall expected that even Bo Xilai would have trouble spinning this one.

Bo donned a pair of spectacles to read perfunctorily from an official statement. 'First, I'll give you a standard response,' he said, without hiding his disdain for having to stoop to the vacuous Party-speak that was standard fare for most of his colleagues, except Premier Wen Jiabao. 'Wang Lijun is being investigated by the relevant central agencies...' Then he set aside his prepared statement, took off his glasses and made eye contact with the journalists who had jammed in to see him, while hundreds more were locked outside.

Bo raised an open hand, as if swearing in a court of law, and told how, 'speaking from my heart', he had never held any national leadership ambitions beyond his work in Chongqing. In the next breath he pointedly revealed that China's national Gini coefficient – the sensitive worldwide inequality measure, which had not been publicly released in a decade – had risen to the alarming level of 0.46, which stood in obvious contrast to the diminishing rich–poor gap he had been boasting of in Chongqing. He brazenly suggested President Hu Jintao should come to Chongqing to personally inspect what he had achieved. Bo was tolling the bell on a social and political crisis and holding himself out as the saviour of the Communist Party, socialism and the nation.

Bo Xilai knew the Party had never had the courage to seriously apply the law to its own children. His performance was an act of defiance worthy of his father, who had been gaoled by the Kuomintang and 'knocked down' twice by his comrades-in-arms and still returned to power and outlived them all. In

1954, when Bo Xilai and the People's Republic were both five years old, Bo's father had been accused of the same character flaws that the son was criticised for now. Bo Yibo, who had been minister of finance, possessed 'bourgeois individualist ideas and working style', he 'likes to make decisions arbitrarily' and colleagues must be wary of his 'arrogance and rashness', said his critics.[2] He was accused of being too far to the right because he had proposed equal tax treatment for private and state-owned firms. Later, early in the Cultural Revolution, Bo Yibo was brutally purged and accused of being a 'capitalist roader'. Neither father nor son allowed themselves to be caught on the liberal side of consensus again.

Bo Yibo led the 1987 conservative attack on China's most liberal and popular leader, Hu Yaobang, opening the post-Mao ideological cleavage that reverberates today. Xi Zhongxun, the father of China's president-in-waiting, Xi Jinping, was the only elder who spoke up in Hu's defence – escalating a rivalry with Bo Yibo that spanned most of his career in government.[3] Hu Yaobang was airbrushed from official history, but the core of the current and incoming leadership have continued to quietly honour Hu Yaobang's legacy. The lesson Bo Xilai learned from his father's bruising career – as victim and then aggressor – was that it was always the reformers who were torn down, while those on the left were forgiven for the sorts of honest mistakes that revolutionaries make.

'If a new capitalist class is created, then we'll really have turned onto a wrong road,' warned Bo Xilai, rising to the climax of his final press conference and echoing the 'capitalist roader' accusation that had once been made against his father. He even recited a popular Mao-era poem: 'Dare to fight for the high ground with these devils; Never give an inch to the overlords.'

'Destroy me if you dare,' he seemed to be saying to his leadership peers, who were no doubt watching every word. He was calculating that those loyal to the memory of Hu Yaobang would not challenge the 25-year ascendancy of conservative political ideology. The stage was set for Vice President Xi Jinping to take the upper hand in his family's six-decade tussle with the House of Bo.

A Dynastic Succession

Bo Xilai publicly railed against 'capitalists' and 'overlords' but in private he was more willing than any of his peers to deal with them. Almost exactly one year earlier, in the days following the 2011 National People's Congress, the US ambassador Jon Huntsman was making his final calls before returning home to run for the Republican presidential nomination. Tensions were high between the world's only superpower and its sole credible challenger.

The next American presidency would be focused on restoring fiscal stability and steering the United States through a crisis of confidence. China's new leadership team, to be selected around Xi Jinping at the 18th Communist Party Congress immediately after the American presidential election, would face an even more daunting task. China's success in steering most of its 1.3 billion people out of poverty and towards modernity seemed to be creating more problems than it was alleviating. The Party was leaning more heavily on its monopoly on violence to increase its control over a better-informed and more assertive citizenry, as it was losing its monopoly on truth. The incoming leaders would need to defend the sixty-year-old communist dictatorship against a democratic tide that was rising inside and outside China.

Bo Xilai had already demonstrated that he understood, better than anybody else, how China was entering a new world of political contestation, where leaders were no longer anointed by the heroes of the communist revolution.[4] The leaders who followed Hu Jintao, whose decade as general secretary would expire at the Party's 18th Congress, would need to convince their peers that they were best able to look after their personal interests and maintain their collective rule over an increasingly engaged and globalised population. The Communist Party was drifting into an era of quasi-democratic internal struggle but it lacked any of the democratic ground rules or institutions that had developed over centuries in the West to mediate the game.

Huntsman, the popular former Governor of Utah, had been an impressive emissary but he had been stepping up his advocacy for political reform and human rights as he prepared for his re-entry into American politics. In March 2011, he was under fire in some sections of the Chinese state media for allegedly encouraging a Tunisian-style 'Jasmine Revolution', because he had turned up with his family to observe an advertised anti-government protest in downtown Beijing. Any protestors who were there that Sunday outside the McDonald's at Wangfujing, Beijing's busiest shopping street, were vastly outnumbered by undercover Chinese security officials, who bustled Huntsman out of the way. From that point on, senior Chinese leaders had flatly refused to see him.

Bo, however, opened his door. Initially they discussed Bo's Chongqing economic model and potential American investment. Bo found the similarities between their ambitions and respective family dynasties at least as intriguing as the differences.

Bo Xilai and Jon Huntsman are uncommonly capable, confident and handsome. They had learned each other's languages at times when it was unfashionable to do so, Bo as a junior high student before the Cultural Revolution and Huntsman as a Mormon missionary. Huntsman is the son of a billionaire industrialist who made his fortune manufacturing clamshell packaging for Big Mac hamburgers. Bo's father, Bo Yibo, emerged from his Cultural Revolution purgatory to regain his position as vice premier and take his place as one of the 'Eight Immortals' of the communist revolution: the group of Mao's close comrades-in-arms led by Deng Xiaoping, who emerged ascendant after Mao's death and oversaw China's opening to the world. And they were each leveraging their inherited privileges to take them towards the political apex of their respective systems.

Bo Xilai is known in China as a 'princeling', or more literally a member of the 'crown prince party', a term that encapsulates the ancient dynastic-communist amalgam he was born into. It was coined in the Hong Kong media in the 1980s to describe the hundreds of children of senior Communist Party leaders who enjoyed an inside track to money, power and great privilege. Princelings themselves, however, detest the label. The progeny of the most exclusive group of founding fathers, like Bo Yibo and Xi Zhongxun, prefer more revolutionary labels like 'red successor'. In the Chinese mutation of communism, Bo was as entitled to inherit his father's political power as Huntsman was to receive his father's money.

A few days after their Beijing meeting, on 21 March 2011, Huntsman flew with his wife, Mary Kaye, to Chongqing to resume the conversation at

Bo's elegant, expansive and colonial-style government guesthouse. High walls and luxuriant gardens allowed for intimate conversation away from the construction noise of this major city in Southwest China, whose economy was growing at an average annual rate of 16 per cent.

Bo Xilai was at his charming and charismatic best. After running through investment opportunities, Bo beckoned the Huntsmans into his private office. The Americans found it reassuring to see the pictures on the office walls presented a history of Bo's photogenic family, rather than the usual trophy shots next to grim-faced Communist Party luminaries. Bo had always been fascinated with photographs of faces, especially his own. 'On some levels they reflect the peoples' innermost worlds, including their thoughts, qualities, and personalities,' he had once written, in a love letter while courting his first wife.[5]

Bo carefully walked the Huntsmans through his family's central role in the Communist Party's story, starting with the 1920s, and explained the significance of some of the photographs. There were pictures of his parents together; his mother with Chairman Mao; himself with the master statesman Premier Zhou Enlai; and his father with what was described as the Deng-era reform team, including a very youthful Hu Jintao. Bo spoke passionately and lovingly about his family's contributions, and he did not evade their hardships. The familiarity of family papered over an otherwise incomprehensible gulf between the secure comforts of the American moneyed elite and the untrammelled power and physical insecurities of China's founding families. The dynastic feuds, between families and within them, and China's sheer political brutality were kept from view.

Bo Xilai is taller than his six siblings, at six foot one, and he appeared younger than his sixty-one years. He has the master politician's gift for reading people and engaging, no matter the class or cultural distance between them. His demeanour can be dignified, with earnest eyes and thin-rimmed reading spectacles, and he possesses a dimpled smile that can light up a room. There is no hint from Bo's appearance that he spent his first five years of adulthood in what was effectively a torture and brainwashing camp. The standard official portrait of Bo's deceased father, Bo Yibo, shows him with a grandfatherly smile and disarming cotton-tufted eyebrows, wearing a Mao jacket buttoned up to the collar. Bo Yibo's earliest memory was of watching his mother give birth to his baby brother only to have to drown him shortly afterwards because there was not enough food to share around. In the civil war, Bo Yibo spent five years in a Kuomintang gaol and then most of

Mao's ten-year Cultural Revolution in purgatory.

Jon Huntsman saw the passion, inquiring intellect and raw charisma that were making Bo Xilai the emerging force in Chinese politics. He didn't see any hint of the Maoist thinking that Bo's enemies and some of his supporters were mobilising against at that very point in time. Mao had simply caused the family too much suffering, thought Huntsman. Members of the Bo clan, however, remained steadfastly loyal to both Mao and the political system that enabled him to happen. 'Chairman Mao is the greatest leader and mentor in the heart of my father,' Bo's younger brother, Bo Xicheng, said after the patriarch's passing in 2007. 'Without Mao, where would we be?'

Bo Xilai's wife, Gu Kailai, who is nine years his junior,[6] played an intimate role in Bo's inner court but was battling illness, depression and paranoia and had withdrawn from public life. Photographs showed her with prominent cheekbones, a small shapely mouth and hair fashionably cut and loosely parted down the middle. She was a successful lawyer who spoke glowingly of the efficiency of the Chinese criminal justice system compared with its procedurally tedious and sometimes 'absurd' American counterpart. 'We don't quibble with words,' she wrote in a 1998 book about her own legal exploits.

'We have a principle called "based on the facts". As long as we know you killed someone, you will be arrested, sentenced and executed.' Her father, a powerful general in his own right, had been imprisoned by his own Party for a dozen years when she was three years old, again for imagined political misdemeanours.

Bo and Gu's beloved son, Bo Guagua, like his parents, had long ignored the Communist Party convention of public humility and total personal secrecy. He keeps impeccably manicured and wears braces, waistcoats and slim-fitting shirts. US infringement records show he drove a brand-new black Porsche Panamera around Harvard University, where he was studying for a Masters in public policy, and friends say he has driven them around Beijing in a red sports car. He played polo, appeared on Chinese chat shows and brought his friend Jackie Chan to speak at Oxford, and even sang with him on stage. His earnest charm, engaging mind and capacity for fun made him the centre of a web of friendships that stretched across three continents – although some found him narcissistic. Friends posted pictures of him wearing glossy red lipstick and partying at Oxford with his shirt off, displaying a physique that might make an Olympic gymnast proud. When he was 'rusticated', for being a wayward student, three officials from the Chinese embassy turned up to see what could be done. Bo Guagua became involved in various ventures, which he says did not involve any profit motive.

Bo Guagua staunchly defended the Communist party and was not the most excessive of China's 'Politbrats'. His father's neo-Maoist supporters were content to look the other way. Guagua's mother calls him 'Little Rabbit', for his birth year in the Chinese zodiac. He called her 'Big Rabbit' in return.[7]

When the Huntsmans stepped further into Bo Xilai's private Chongqing office, they were surprised to find 24-year-old Bo Guagua, China's most eligible bachelor, seated in the corner and waiting for an introduction. He looks almost exactly as his father did at the same age. According to a source who was in the room, after talking about Guagua's studies in the US, Bo Xilai turned to his guests and asked, 'I believe you have daughters about the same age?' Mary Kaye wrote down the email address of their daughters, according to a second source who was present. Bo Guagua provided his email in return. A month later, Bo Guagua and Mary Anne Huntsman met with friends at the classy Nobu Japanese restaurant in Beijing and later proceeded to drinks at an exclusive bar. There are conflicting accounts of how, exactly, the evening panned out,[8] but it's clear that the junior Bo was eager to impress. The intriguing and subversive possibility of a dynastic family alliance between the United States and China did not last long.

One year later, when Jon Huntsman failed to gain the support he needed to stay in the presidential nomination race, Mary Anne and her sisters signed off on their @Jon2012girls Twitter campaign with a promise of more to come: 'Many flames burn out in politics, our dad's has just been ignited. What an incredible journey for our family. Thanks for all the support!'

The losers in Chinese politics, however, do not fall so gently. The Bo family entered 2012 insulated from law and public scrutiny, but now it is subject to the whims of Communist Party justice. Bo Xilai is in the process of being purged, without access to lawyers or friends or any hope of a transparent trial. Bo's wife, Gu Kailai, is languishing in a gaol as a common criminal, after being convicted of murdering one of her son's important English patrons. The case against her was 'irrefutable', said the official Xinhua News Agency, before the trial began. And Bo Guagua is marooned in the US, apparently studying to enter law school, and pondering the family's proven capacity for political resurrection.

The purge of Bo Xilai has been so far mild

compared with the days when political rivals were tortured, exploded in plane crashes or imprisoned and left to die in their own vomit. The novelty of this one is that it is being acted out in the midst of China's information revolution and in front of an increasingly prosperous, educated and sceptical population. The political explosion of Bo Xilai is blowing open the black box of Chinese politics and laying bare a world of staggering brutality, corruption, hypocrisy and fragility. For the first time, the webs of power and money that bind and also divide China's red aristocracy are being exposed for the world to see. The demise of Bo Xilai has opened cleavages in the Party along factional, ideological and personal lines. The battle over how to frame his legacy has become a proxy war for China's future. The scars that are opening up date back to the Cultural Revolution, when Bo Xilai and his colleagues were coming of age.

The Red Terror

The Bo brothers attended China's most exclusive high school at a time when it was stacked with princelings – known then as 'children of high cadres' – who were anxious to live up to the revolutionary exploits of their parents. In the mid 1960s, the privileged children at Beijing No. 4 Middle School were among the first to respond to Mao's growing emphasis on 'class struggle' and the need to nurture a new generation of 'revolutionary successors'. Bo's elder brother, Bo Xiyong, had been at the fore of a movement that had succeeded in scrapping the old meritocratic national examination system, which had been forcing children of red revolutionaries to compete on an equal footing with those from 'bad' intellectual families. 'A Red C is better than a White A,' was a popular slogan at the time.

In the late northern spring of 1966, Chairman Mao ignited the decade of orchestrated carnage known as the Cultural Revolution by mobilising students into militant Red Guards and turning them against his own establishment. The orchestrated violence and humiliations further elevated Mao's position and destroyed his imagined rivals, even though he already enjoyed god-like status. His ideal of perpetual struggle and revolution required a roll call of enemy targets, in and outside the Party, to mobilise the rest of the Party and the masses against. The period was the ultimate display of personal power, removed from any semblance of law or process. One of the Party's darkest secrets is how the first rampages of Mao's Cultural Revolution were led almost exclusively by princeling children who are today rising to the strategic heights of power.

One of Bo's classmates, whose father was a People's Liberation Army general, invented a rhyming two-line ditty that defined the hereditary class battle lines and became the anthem for the early princeling Red Guard movement: 'The father's a hero, the son's a good lad; the father's a reactionary, the son's a bastard.'[9] Bo Xiyong fought to be head of the school's Cultural Revolution Group, according to his princeling rivals, but was forced to settle for deputy.

Bo Xilai was shy and studious compared to his athletic elder brother and his boisterous younger brother, Bo Xicheng.[10] In his early school years he had swum against the current by joining the English language stream, when most of his peers were studying Russian. Peers considered him to be the brightest and quietest of the Bo boys.[11] They say he shared in the class bigotry but – contrary to myth – was not a leader among the children who rampaged on campus and in the neighbourhood, rounding up students, school administrators and others deemed to come from bad family backgrounds.[12] It was a formative experience, all the same.

China's most prestigious playground began to resemble a scene from *Lord of the Flies*. Victims were branded 'cow ghosts and snake devils' – a Buddhist term referring to the evil spirits in hell that had gained currency in the *People's Daily* – and they were paraded through the schoolyard to be beaten and abused. On 4 August, the student leaders of the school's Cultural Revolution Group directed prisoners into an old canteen, initially for their protection, but the sanctuary degenerated into a hall of torture and ritual humiliation. Student leaders recall how they forced their prisoners, including the school principal, to stand in choir formation and sing loudly and in tune: 'I am one of the cow ghosts and snake devils… I am guilty, I should die, the masses should smash me to pieces and pound me into mash.'[13] According to witnesses, including the chief prison guard, a popular slogan was written on the wall in human blood: 'Long Live the Red Terror!' Prisoners were beaten and lashed until bone could be seen through lacerated flesh. Several prisoners died in the cafeteria-gaol and four teachers committed suicide outside it.[14] 'We could sense the stench of blood, like a slaughterhouse,' says Yang Fan, a friend and classmate of Bo Xicheng, who later co-founded the *Utopia* website, which played an important role in Bo Xilai's ascendancy. 'This is why Chinese people hate princelings even today.'

Princeling veterans of that era, now aged in their sixties, including the Bo siblings, seldom discuss this early and most brutal period of the Cultural Revolution, which others call 'bloody August' or 'the red terror'. But they do keep alive memories of how Mao turned his Cultural Revolution mercilessly against them later in the year.

Most of Mao's top comrades-in-arms were targeted, including Bo Yibo, who was a close sub-ordinate of Mao's 'No. 1 Capitalist Roader' enemy, President Liu Shaoqi. Only months earlier, in June 1966, Bo Yibo had cryptically warned a Tsinghua University Red Guard leader about the dangers of taking the revolution too far in China's fickle system: 'A circle consists of a left semi-circle and a right semi-circle. Going too far to the left, you end up on the right.'[15] Events soon showed that even the most experienced players, like Bo Yibo, could be caught off balance in a system where the political winds could turn 180 degrees overnight. The Red Guard leader told Bo Yibo he was a fat old man and later led his public persecution.

Bo Yibo was captured in December, when he was recuperating from illness with his wife Hu Ming in the southern city of Guangzhou,[16] and the following month dragged to Beijing's Workers' Stadium with his head shackled in an iron rack. In front of a vast and seething crowd, he was accused of opposing Chairman Mao, taking the capitalist road and being a traitor because of a retrospective crime committed thirty-five years earlier.[17] Bo Yibo showed a reck-lessly defiant streak that his children inherited. 'I am not a traitor! I am a member of the Communist Party,' he shouted to the heaving crowd. He had his head thrust forward, his face pulled up and his arms wrenched high behind his back in what was becom-ing known as the 'jet plane' position. A series of iconic photos shows another stubborn revolutionary leader, Xi Jinping's father Xi Zhongxun, standing next to Bo Yibo in an identical predicament. For once they found themselves on the same side of the Party's internal battle lines. In yet another twist that informs the political battles today, the Red Guards who captured Bo Yibo were from the Beijing Geological Institute – where the current premier and Bo's contemporary nemesis, Wen Jiabao, was employed as a postgraduate researcher and was actively involved in campus politics. It is not clear whether Premier Wen personally played a role in Bo Yibo's 'struggle' sessions.[18]

Bo Yibo endured months of starvation and days of blistering heat without sleep or water. Frequently they beat him into unconsciousness. 'Most unbearably painful in all of this was when my arms were being twisted out of joint,' wrote Bo on a scrap of newspaper in August 1967, which somehow emerged for publication in the 1980s.[19] Bo's torturers reported to their superiors that they had subjected the revolutionary veteran to more than a hundred 'struggle' sessions, but still he 'remained stubborn in his resistance'. Bo Yibo thought often of his beloved wife, Bo Xilai's mother Hu Ming, who he hadn't seen since they were captured and she was bundled onto a northbound train by a Red Guard in January. He had no way to know that before the train reached its destination she had 'committed suicide for fear of punishment', to use the official euphemism of the time, or was 'persecuted to death', to use the contemporary language of their daughter.[20]

Bo Yibo sustained himself by staring at photos of Hu Ming and their seven children. In the summer of 1967, he was permitted to write and he urged his children to 'stand up straight' and 'blaze for yourself a correct path of a revolutionary life'. His life had become 'acceptable', he lied, and he apologised for the misfortune he knew he had brought upon them.[21] The family memory passed down to Bo Guagua was that Bo Yibo was purged for promoting market reforms, his maternal grandfather for sheltering intellectuals and his maternal grandmother for being too liberal – and that the family's long-term interests were paramount, no matter what the short-term cost. The idea that any of the family could have been perpetrators or aggressors was not easily entertained.

In 1967, the status of Bo Xilai and his two brothers at No. 4 plunged, in parallel with their parents, and children from lesser class backgrounds relished their revenge. 'The oppressors became the oppressed; the attackers were attacked,' recalls a fellow student, Duan Ruoshi, who believes the Bo brothers suffered extra punishment for their 'arrogance'.[22] The Bos and their top-ranking princeling friends – a son of President Liu Shaoqi and two sons of Beijing municipal Party boss Peng Zhen –'suddenly went from wearing army uniforms with red armbands, all high and mighty, to walking dejected along the walls and trying to avoid eye contact,' says Duan. The new band of Red Guards from ordinary families forced Bo Xilai and his two brothers into jet-plane positions, thrusting their heads forward and wrenching back their hair. Even class foes remarked on how tough they were. 'Despite the shouts of condemnation from all sides, Bo Yibo's sons exuded defiance and writhed their bodies against their oppressors,' says Duan.[23] Bo Xilai and his two brothers spent the next five years at a princeling concentration camp on the northern outskirts of Beijing.

The Bo brothers have never spoken publicly about their ordeals at Camp 789. According to other veterans, however, conditions were barbaric. They suffered extreme sleep deprivation, filthy conditions, semi-starvation and beatings. Veterans recall how the inmates would devour frogs and sparrows that flew in through barred windows. It was there, in the evenings after forced labour, that Bo Xilai memorised reams of Mao Zedong quotations, because there was little else to do.

Powerful myths have evolved about Bo's school-yard antics that purportedly explain the man he became. Some of Bo's peers tell a story that he helped to beat two people to death while a member of an organisation called Liandong, echoing a discredited story that was published by a newspaper run by the outlawed religious group, Falun Gong.[24] Many claim that Bo committed the ultimate betrayal of Chinese traditional values by physically beating his father to the point that he broke his ribs.[25] But nobody, it seems, can present a plausible account of when or where these events might have happened. His closest classmates say they didn't. 'It couldn't have happened,' says the student leader of Bo Xilai's class, Fu Yang, who was close to Bo as a student but fell out recently when Bo arrested Li Zhuang, an employee at his law firm. Fu Yang's father, Peng Zhen, was deposed as Beijing Party chief at the onset of the Cultural Revolution and later rehabilitated to rank alongside Bo Yibo as one of the 'Eight Immortals'. (Bo Xilai later married the daughter of Peng Zhen's successor as Beijing Party chief). The children had been held in jet-plane positions alongside each other at No. 4. Fu Yang says Bo Yibo was 'struck down' while in Guangzhou and taken directly by Red Guards to his detention in Beijing, while Bo Xilai was taken to the 789 prison camp. The camp was established for the purpose of having princeling children denounce their fallen parents, he said, but beating them was a different matter. 'He didn't have any opportunity to see his father, so how could he have beaten him?' And, shooting down the myth that Bo was an adolescent murderer, he added: 'The Liandong matter must be fabricated.' [26]

After the initial Cultural Revolution years of intense violence, most elite students and princelings were exiled to the countryside, where they encountered the freedom to think more independently and mix beyond their usual peer groups. Many, including incoming president Xi Jinping, look back nostalgically on this time among the peasants in the 'classroom' of ordinary life. Bo Xilai, however, spent those years in inhumane confinement. He 'skipped his class,' says a fellow princeling, whose former husband was incarcerated with Bo at 789, but who declined to speak on the record. She believes this was the formative moment when Bo learnt little more than how to torture, abuse and persecute. 'It left a very evil mark in their lives,' she said. 'Their capacity for self-examination is very limited.'[27] Fu Yang, in contrast, who was Bo's class monitor and whose brother was also imprisoned in Camp 789, argues there was nothing about Bo's adolescent ordeals that presaged his later excesses.

After Mao died in 1976, his old comrades-in-arms were gradually brought back from purgatory to oversee China's epic journey of 'opening and reform'. Following all of the 'anguish and misfortune' the founding fathers had brought upon their children, as Bo Yibo had put it, the least they could do was give them a hand up in their careers. They gave each other's children an inside path into China's leading universities and positioned them in crucial career-building positions. Bo Xilai enrolled to study international history at Peking University in 1977 and then shifted after two years to journalism at the Chinese Academy of Social Sciences. (While Bo's entrance to the prestigious university relied in part on his father pulling strings he made it known that he, unlike Xi Jinping, had also sat one of the world's most competitive entrance examinations.) After graduating, Bo was given a plum entry-level job in the Party's Central Secretariat. Then he was assigned to the northern port city of Dalian in 1984, as a deputy county Party boss, which his first wife attributes to her father's powerful local connections. It was there that he began his climb up the provincial hierarchy away from the intense competition of Beijing. Many princelings never let go of their adolescent assertions that the country was rightfully theirs.

In the 1980s, Bo Yibo played a crucial intermediary and spear-carrier role for the new paramount leader, Deng Xiaoping. Bo Yibo's political importance grew as China's increasingly market-oriented economy and liberalising social environment began to clash with the elders' demand for absolute political control. In 1987, Bo Yibo chaired the Orwellian-named 'Democratic Party Life' meeting, which ambushed and deposed the popular liberal Party chief, Hu Yaobang. Bo Yibo's personal reputation never recovered from his attacks on the man who had courageously reversed his own record as a 'traitor' and rehabilitated his career. Hu had also rehabilitated Vice President Xi Jinping's father, Xi Zhongxun,[28] and in the early 1980s brought Xi Zhongxun to a senior leadership position in the Party's Central Secretariat, where they became close friends. The elder Xi cemented his public reputation as a loyal, decent and reformist leader by being the only elder who spoke up in Hu's defence at the torrid week-long Party Life meeting. He had been furious that his fellow elders had disregarded their own laws.[29]

Another who was scarred by the 1987 ordeal was Wen Jiabao, the teacher's son, who Hu Yaobang had just promoted to run his General Office, a position akin to cabinet secretary. Another Hu protégé whose career was nearly bumped off course was the son of a tea merchant, Hu Jintao. In 1986, Hu Yaobang had told the Australian ambassador at the time that

Hu Jintao would one day be the general secretary of the Communist Party of China.[30] In 1988, Bo Yibo, who had headed the Party's personnel work for the 13th Party Congress, shifted Hu Jintao to Tibet in what then seemed like a dead-end posting.

Hu Yaobang's death in March 1989 triggered the protests of Tiananmen. Bo Yibo placed himself at the forefront of another ruthless purge, this time of Hu's reformist successor, Zhao Ziyang. Bo joined Deng Xiaoping and the fellow elders to declare martial law against the protestors, leaving the bloodiest stain in modern Chinese history. Bo Yibo moved to have Wen Jiabao purged from his job running the General Office, according to a source whose father was a minister at the time, but other elders intervened. Even today Premier Wen Jiabao, President Hu Jintao, Vice President Xi Jinping and Vice Premier Wen Jiabao regularly honour the widow of Hu Yaobang, who lives across the road from the leadership compound at Zhongnanhai.[31] Their entanglements with Bo Yibo in the 1980s have greatly complicated relations with his son, Bo Xilai

Through the 1990s, Bo Yibo emerged gradually from the shadow of an ageing Deng and intervened at crucial junctures to bolster the command of the new Party chief and president, Jiang Zemin, who he had helped bring to power. In 1992, when Deng made his famous Southern Tour to re-start economic reforms, and believed Jiang was dragging his feet, Bo Yibo played a possibly decisive role in stopping him from sacking Jiang. 'Not for the third time,' Bo told Deng, arguing that dumping three Party chiefs in five years would be excessive.[32] A decade later, when Jiang was handing over to his successor, President Hu Jintao, Bo played a crucial role in enabling Jiang to retain substantial power by staying on as head of the People's Liberation Army.[33] In the Chinese tradition of patronage and reciprocity, Jiang was deeply in Bo Yibo's debt.

President Jiang repaid Bo Yibo by looking after the career of his son. In 1993, Bo Xilai was appointed mayor of Dalian, the port to China's rustbelt Northeast. The younger Bo reciprocated by providing Jiang with a comfortable beach house, an hours' drive from Dalian, where Jiang would often visit.[34] He erected a huge photo of President Jiang in the main city square, despite a post-Mao ban on such 'personality cult' trappings. He outdid other regional leaders in the political and often brutal struggle against Jiang's imagined internal enemy, the 'evil cult' Falun Gong.[35]

In 1999, Bo Xilai was promoted from mayor to Party secretary of Dalian. In 2001, he was again promoted, to governor of the surrounding province,

Liaoning. He locked his loyalties to Jiang, who had come to command a powerful coterie of protégés he brought with him to Beijing, labelled by the Hong Kong media as the 'Shanghai Gang'. Beyond Jiang, Bo demonstrated a willingness to burn old friendships, forge new networks across factional, ideological and organisational lines and loudly indulge his personal idiosyncrasies. It was in Dalian and Liaoning province that Bo assembled his 'inner circle' and tested the transformative governance methods that would later be unleashed in Chongqing.

The Prince of Dalian

After the liberalising 1980s, when peasants were
among the first to see their incomes swell and the
industrial economy was driven by township entrepreneurs, China clicked into a new gear of urban-centric
and state-driven capitalism. 'Development' was the
mantra and municipal leaders demonstrated their
commitment to that ideal by revamping coastal cities.

As soon as Bo became mayor of Dalian, the main
port for the old heavy industrial base of northeast
China, he set to work touting for investors, widening
the streets, erecting shiny tall buildings and renovat-
ing prominent public places. One of his first steps
was to change the name of Stalin Square to People's
Square and establish China's first all-female mounted
police unit to tour the newly beautified square each
morning. The tall, slender and smartly uniformed

policewomen – with an average age of twenty-three – became tourist attractions in their own right.[36] 'Investors look at a city and judge it by how it looks,' Bo would later say.[37]

Bo was enamoured with Europe, particularly the cool climes of Switzerland and Scotland. He was fond of the acres of manicured evergreen grass and the quirky painted fibreglass cows he admired on his frequent visits to Zurich[38], so he replicated them in Dalian. Born in the Year of the Ox, Bo took the cow to be his city's emblem. He introduced German-style beer festivals and international fashion shows. Dalian was bulldozed, re-built and polished into a work of shiny modernity. It was his personal trophy town. It wasn't long before he could control the colour of the water fountains and the accompanying soundtracks (he liked mournful Scottish ballads) via a console on the balcony of his 200-square-metre office, which overlooked People's Square.[39]

Bo proved to be equally charming and at ease drinking Korean investors under the table in Dalian's ribald karaoke bars, dining with the families of Japanese and Western investors, and honouring Chinese peasants and businessmen in his home at Chinese New Year. 'His dress, his posture, his style, his charisma, his people skills – it was a bit like Bill Clinton when he walked into a room, he had an aura about him,' said Lloyd Donaldson, the Australian manager of the city's most luxurious hotel, the Japanese-owned Swissotel. Donaldson, who knew Bo well, wondered at the time whether Bo's British-accented English, love of Swiss food and open-minded curiosity for all things Western might put him offside with Party conservatives. 'He wanted to influence Dalian with European and western values.'

As well as pulling capital and expertise from neighbouring South Korea and Japan, Bo targeted local businessmen to cultivate. He worked closely with Wang Jianlin, the founder of a local real estate company called Dalian Wanda Group, which now owns forty-nine shopping centres across the country and cinema chains as far away as the US. As soon as Bo became mayor of Dalian, his friend Wang stepped in to sponsor the local soccer team, turning it into political gold by purchasing the players it needed to dominate the national league. Bo also helped a well-spoken young entrepreneur, Xu Ming, to become one of the country's most powerful businessmen, initially by assisting him gain key construction contracts to renovate the Dalian streetscape at the age of twenty-one.[40] In 2000, when Wang tired of the match-fixing in Chinese football, Bo made sure Xu was standing by to take over the local team. Bo's backing has helped both businessmen, Wang and Xu, recently climb into the top ten US dollar billionaires. Wang has managed to successfully diversify his patrons and is now listed as the richest man in China, while Xu Ming has entrenched himself more deeply in the family's inner court.

Bo took heed of Mao's Cultural Revolution instruction that you need a little *wu* (violence) as well as *wen* (culture) to get things done. Bo promoted his former cook and driver to be his city security chief. He also brought on board an intelligence official, Yu Junshi, who had been ejected from the PLA after a mishap in Thailand, in part to keep an eye on others in his circle.[41] And he continued to cultivate the young businessman Xu Ming who, in turn, enmeshed Bo and his wife in his own expanding network.

Liaoning province at the turn of the millennium was the epicentre of history's largest redundancy program, which saw nearly fifty million Chinese workers laid off from state-related enterprises in the decade to 2003. [42] Unemployed middle-aged men could be seen each morning gathering at Liaoning's street corners, hoping for work, in contrast to the dynamic export hubs of China's eastern and southern coastline. The mass privatisation and restructuring of 'iron rice bowl' enterprises in China's northeast rustbelt triggered a backlash against China's perceived 'neo-liberal' turn, particularly within the intellectual New Left and conservative segments of the Party. Bo was combative towards entrepreneurs who made a difficult economic situation worse by taking their capital elsewhere.

Liaoning was the production base for China's largest private carmaker, Brilliance China Automotive, which had a joint venture with BMW. Its owner, Yang Rong, owed his success in part to a murky ownership deal that stemmed from top-level PLA connections. Bo was furious when Yang exacerbated the economic dislocation by moving to set up a huge new factory in Shanghai rather than Liaoning. He responded by nationalising Yang's US$700 million stake and charging him with embezzlement, prompting Yang to seek exile in the United States.[43] It was the first hint of Bo's later uncompromising stance against private capital.

Bo engaged selectively with private entrepreneurs, however, particularly his close associates. Many believe that Bo assisted Xu Ming gain a ten per cent stake in what became one of China's most profitable financial firms, China Pacific Insurance, which required cutting through webs of administrative approvals.[44] Xu invested in Bo's network as he grew more powerful and used his money and charm to produce relationships otherwise beyond Bo's reach. Xu Ming became close friends with Premier Wen

Jiabao's daughter, Wen Ruchun, travelling with her to Europe and doing business with Wen family associates.[45] Xu also invested in the consultancy firm operated by Bo's wife, Gu Kailai. Bo ordered the local newspaper, the *Dalian Daily*, to build a ¥500 million new headquarters, for which Bo's wife did the legal work and took a twenty per cent stake in the construction firm, according to *Dalian Daily* journalist, Jiang Weiping, who was gaoled for reporting the connection and other stories about Bo family corruption.[46] Bo Xilai, Gu Kailai and Xu Ming proved to be a formidable combination.

Gu Kailai is Bo's second wife. He had met his first wife, Li Danyu, in a different era, during the Cultural Revolution in 1975, when his family was still in purgatory. Li's father, Li Xuefeng, had been Beijing Party chief in the early years of the Cultural Revolution.[47] Li Danyu still speaks admiringly of Bo Xilai's early commitment to revolutionary ideals. 'We believed we needed to save the rest of the world from the hell of capitalism,' she said[48] He courted her with letters written in the language of revolutionary romance and wrote her poems that copied the style of Chairman Mao. Bo married Li on September 1976, the month Mao died, and they had a son the following year. But their relationship turned bitter as Bo stepped forth into the new world of opening and reform. He redoubled his efforts to master English, his family's fortunes soared, and her family became a political liability as the new post-Mao leadership left her father languishing in purgatory. Her father had still not been rehabilitated when he told her he wanted to leave her, in 1981, just days before Deng Xiaoping's epic resolution on history that officially closed the Mao era. Li believes Bo had already become a university dance partner with her sister-in-law, the glamorous and adventurous Gu Kailai, nine years his junior. Gu was a fellow member of the red aristocracy, the daughter of a general from the anti-Japanese war who was returning to powerful positions in the post-Mao era. Gu's elder sister was married to the brother of Bo's wife, Li Danyu. Li blames Gu for ending her marriage.

Gu Kailai studied law and international politics and polished her English at Peking University. She told state media that she saw the same idealism in Bo as she appreciated in her father. Bo and Gu were married in 1986 and Bo Guagua was born in December the following year. In Dalian, her brains, charm and beauty made her seem like the 'Jackie Kennedy of China', according to an American lawyer who worked with her on a case in the 1990s, for which she had been hired by her husband's government.[49] The work involved her flying to the US to instruct local lawyers in a successful appeal against an earlier decision to penalise Chinese companies for intellectual property theft. In 1998 she made a splash in the legal fraternity with a self-flattering book on the case, *Uphold Justice in America*, which legal peers considered to be over-the-top because she had relied entirely on American lawyers. A subsequent television series depicts a no-nonsense lawyer who fell in love with a handsome politician. Her business cards from the time give her English name as Horus, after the Egyptians' falcon-headed god of sky, war and hunting. Her law firm, Horus L. Kai, and a consultancy with a similar name played gatekeeper roles for doing business in the town.

Bo and Gu were united by their shared ambition to cement the family's dynastic place in Chinese history and smooth their son's passage into the English education system and the global aristocracy beyond. But after the early years of adventure, the formidable couple didn't always act in tandem, as he became further consumed with his pursuit of power. Bo kept nocturnal hours, channelling his prodigious energy into politics and related play. He apparently had a voracious appetite for younger women, although no doubt some of this was myth. Amid the swirling rumours and tabloid tales, a defamation writ filed in July in the Hong Kong High Court denied that Xu

Ming paid ¥100 million for Bo to procure the sexual services of Zhang Ziyi, the star of *Crouching Tiger, Hidden Dragon*.

Bo channelled enormous financial opportunities to useful allies but there's little evidence that he lined his personal pockets. His father loathed money and refused to handle it. Witnesses say they overheard arguments where Bo accused his wife of getting too greedy, although he did nothing to stop his officials and entrepreneurs continuing to shower her with favours. Money, for Bo, was a resource to be channelled and converted into political capital. Gu's gatekeeping role in business helped in this regard.

Through the 1990s, Bo Guagua was largely raised by his grandparents in Beijing. His besotted grandfather, Bo Yibo, gave him his unusual name, which means 'watermelon'. But, unlike most Chinese, Guagua never relinquished the childhood nickname in favour of a more conventional one. Guagua told his mother he felt 'empty' and 'unsatisfied' at his local primary school. The family took the extraordinary step – given conventions and constraints on leaders' families at the time – of charting a new life for him in England when he was just eleven, in 1999. He landed in London with his mother and found himself lost without doting grandparents, attentive maids and cultural reference points. He didn't speak the language, he'd rarely been away from Chinese food and he'd always had all the comforts he could think of. 'This isn't fit to live in,' he told his mother, as they entered one of their many temporary homes.[50] Gu Kailai did what she could to guide his way through an alien world. She enrolled him in an English language school at the seaside town of Bournemouth, providing an almost typical immigrant experience. He studied hard.

Gu arrived at Bournemouth via a circle of local and foreign relationships that assembled around her husband. First among these contacts was a French architect, Patrick Devillers, with whom she set up a consultancy and shared a residence in town. It is likely they had a romantic relationship, according to the British press. Devillers played a peripheral role in Gu's bizarre purchase of an oversized helium balloon that she admired at Bournemouth and wanted to replicate as a tourist gimmick at Dalian. According to the British vendor, Giles Hall, she tried to overpay by 200 000 pounds, with a mix of public and private money, so he could sort out her son's school fees. After Hall refused, 'she said if any of us turned up in China she would get us locked up,' he told *The Times*. 'In Dalian they were all-powerful. Everyone was scared to death of her there.' Money and favours flowed, without necessary lining the family's personal accounts.

Bo Guagua gained a place at Papplewick School, with fees of 22 000 pounds per year, and they upgraded their accommodation. His mother and Devillers jointly purchased two London apartments now worth 3 million pounds, through a family company represented by Gu's sister. Bo Guagua upgraded to Harrow School, with its huge waiting list and 30 000-pound annual fees. Harrow was Guagua's springboard into Oxford University's famous Philosophy, Politics and Economics degree. Bo Xilai, Gu Kailai and their inner circle assisted their son to enter and navigate the kind of challenging and horizon-expanding education that few of his mainland contemporaries have had access to.

Bo Xilai's father continued to worked tirelessly to smooth the family's future. Within four hours of the death of Xi Jinping's father, which occurred at 5.34 a.m., 24 May 2002, the Xi family received an unexpected inter-generational olive branch from the 94-year-old Bo Yibo. The ageing warrior had written a self-deprecating poetic couplet, which quoted from an exchange with Mao half a century earlier, when Mao was reading a report from Xi Zhongxun and had asked for Bo's thoughts. Bo had described Xi in clichéd and slightly patronising terms – 'young and promising' – but Mao firmly put him in his place. Xi, who Mao's forces had once rescued from being buried alive, had been 'tempered by fire', said Mao, alluding to the furnace of immortality that had forged the Monkey King.[51] In quoting those four characters of Mao's – *luhuo chunqing* – Bo Yibo had expertly built a bridge between the children, however shaky, to pursue their common interests.

In 2004, after two decades in Liaoning province, and just after his father had helped Jiang retain enormous power after his ostensible retirement, Bo Xilai was promoted to the national stage as minister of commerce. The position was a step up, although the 25-member Politburo remained beyond Bo's reach. As commerce minister he met daily with international statesmen and business chiefs, who tended to be either awed by his presence or dismayed by his frequent refusal to read briefing notes, in a country where his peers tended to learn them all by rote. There were no serving Chinese leaders who could speak English so fluently or count so many foreign leaders as friends. In January 2007, Bo's father, the last of the revolutionary 'immortals', passed away. Bo Xilai lost his most important backer but the family's powerful patronage networks remained in place, along with some dangerous rivalries. At the end of 2007, Bo Xilai lost his campaign at the 17th Party Congress to be a vice premier, thanks in part to tension with the incumbent in that position.[52] He had not, at that stage, resumed the family enmity with Premier Wen Jiabao, according to business associates. He was promoted into the Politburo but exiled 1500 kilometres from the capital to Chongqing where, perhaps they thought, he was less likely to make trouble. Xi Jinping, Wen Jiabao and Hu Jintao all had workable relations with Bo Xilai, but none could feel at ease with him.

Bo arrived in Chongqing at a moment of national validation. Coverage of the deadly Tibet race riots of March 2008, the acrimonious Olympic torch relay and then the spectacular Beijing Olympics in August of that year all played into a narrative of a resurgent Chinese power overcoming resistance from the hegemonic West. The Party-state told a credible story of leading the nation to overcome 'a century of humiliations' at the hands of foreign imperial powers. During the Olympics, China shot to the top of the gold-medal tables, leaping ahead of the US. And then, as the rich world was struck down with the misleadingly labelled Global Financial Crisis, the Party was able to use its uniquely powerful levers to launch history's greatest economic stimulus package and insulate China. Chinese state power had rarely looked more attractive.

And yet, after such giddy success, the nation felt strangely adrift. The Party had lost the last of the great elders who had created and anchored it – Bo's own father – and it was groping for a new story to bind itself together and continue to justify its monopoly on power. Bo Xilai was early to sense and the first to exploit China's simmering sense of injustice and alienation. China's young people had worked themselves out of poverty to encounter a spiritual void that they yearned to fill. Many of their parents, who had grown up immersed in the ideals of socialism, grew nostalgic for the times when everybody seemed equal, albeit equally poor. A vast gulf was opening up between ordinary citizens and Party officials, their relatives and associates, who had bribed and ingratiated their ways into the system. Party insiders were subject to no restraints while outsiders were shown no empathy. Violent organised crime was both commonplace and indistinguishable from the official establishment. Despite the legendary entrepreneurial spirits of so many Chinese and an age-old acceptance that success revolved around *guanxi* – the ubiquitous term for relationships involving reciprocal obligations – anyone who succeeded in amassing great wealth was presumed to have done so through nefarious means.

The Chongqing Model

When Bo landed as the Communist Party chief of Chongqing at the end of 2007, he spent a year surveying the unfamiliar terrain. The sweltering, smog-shrouded metropolis is centred on a great rock at the juncture of the Jialing and Yangtze rivers. It was once the wartime retreat for Chiang Kai-shek, for whom mountains and mist provided protection from the occupying Japanese. In a similar vein, Chairman Mao moved munitions factories and heavy industry to Chongqing and other inland hide-aways in the 1960s, as they would be further from a Soviet nuclear attack. In 1997, the city was elevated to a province-level municipality. Seven million of Chongqing's thirty-two million people are con-centrated in the metropolis and the rest are spread through the Yangtze River valley across a land area the size of Austria. Chongqing was the centre of a new 'Go West' strategy, designed to spread China's industrialisation and rising prosperity from the shiny coastal cities to the impoverished hinterland.

Bo mapped the city's channels of patronage and nodes of political and financial power, and quietly planted his people. He absorbed the Hu-Wen Administration's renewed emphasis on inequality, and its ambivalence to private capital, and tacked hard to the left. He reached out to descendants of the same Mao family that had persecuted his father and killed his mother. He exploited the growing public resentment by resurrecting the old class enemy, the bourgeoisie, thereby re-animating the Party apparatus and a large portion of 'the masses' by proffering a common enemy to fight against. He wrapped himself in the nostalgia of the revolutionary era, implicitly pointing to the ideals and glories of his father and also the other children of the revolution, like Xi Jinping. He dusted off the old Mao-era songs and quotations he had learned by heart during the five years he spent in prison during the Cultural Revolution. He even banned commercial advertising on his city's television station and filled it with 24-hour 'red' revolutionary programming. His 'sing red' campaign brought socialist ideology and mass movements to Chongqing on a scale that hadn't been seen since the Cultural Revolution. He sent 200 000 officials 'down to the countryside' to learn from the people, in tribute to what Mao had done before him. He pushed a wave of 'red culture' across the city and eventually the nation, and it seemed to work. It was the political *modus operandi* he had grown up with and which people of his generation understood. He seemed to remind members of the Communist Party of their raison d'être.

Bo packaged his economic program as 'red GDP'– alluding to an ideal of socialist equality – as mountains were bulldozed and valleys filled in order to build millions of units of affordable housing. Bo produced bold targets to dramatically reduce the rich–poor gap in his city, while in the rest of the country it was blowing out to be the most extreme in Asia. He laid a latticework of new highways across the municipality and even connected it to Europe by rail. He personally did the deals that enticed global companies to set up and expand huge manufacturing operations – including Hewlett-Packard, Samsung, Ford, BASF, Foxconn – to the point that he could boast that the city produced a third of the world's laptop computers. During Bo's four years, Chongqing's GDP growth was near to the highest in the country, averaging about sixteen per cent. And to complement the roaring and purportedly egalitarian economy, he launched a 'green' program with such gusto and ambitious targets that it reminded some of Mao's Great Leap Forward.

Details were easily submerged in the excitement. Few rural residents seemed to appreciate their new affordable housing, which many received in exchange for being evicted from their rural land. His officials were uprooting the city's great banyan trees like weeds and replacing them with so many grown ginkgos – Bo's favourite – that he sent nationwide prices as high as ¥300 000 a tree. The 2010 tree-planting budget was US$1.5 billion, ten times the budget for renovating rural schools (and which was meant to be a priority project after damage from the Sichuan earthquake).[53] Much of the city's breakneck growth was fuelled by transfers and loans from the rest of the country. The city's bank debt more than doubled in four years.[54]

But still he raised hopes that the Party could overcome its own calcification and petty bureaucratic self-interest to mobilise the nation for a higher cause. He showed how the Party-state could get things done when the right people were in charge. On one level he was honouring the 'harmonious society' ethos of the President Hu and Premier Wen, and may have received their initial support. But he soon made their rhetoric look ineffectual and even lame by comparison.

Bo spun astonishingly complex webs of loyalty and patronage through the Party and its red-blood aristocracy. He was forever making introductions and performing personalised favours. He cultivated the networks of his long-time political patron, former president Jiang Zemin, and extended his princeling networks deep inside the military and across the strategic heights of power. Before engineering the introduction of his son, Bo Guagua, to Mary Anne Huntsman, he had reportedly matched him with Chen Xiaodan, the granddaughter of Chen Yun, another of the Eight Immortals, who had been making a splash in Italian designer dresses at Parisian debutante balls. Their dalliance became the first romance of the red aristocracy to make a public splash, after photographs circulated on the internet showing them holidaying together in Tibet. The Bos and the Chens were bedding down a three-generation family alliance that extended even to Bo's minders asking British diplomats to pay special attention to Chen Xiaodan's tourist visa at the start of this year, according to officials involved. Chen's father, Chen Yuan, who heads the China Development Bank, was more than willing to reciprocate. His bank wrote ¥212 billion in new loans to Chongqing development projects in the first thirty months of Bo Xilai's tenure, according to a collation of figures on the bank's website, which is roughly ten times the average rate of the previous decade.[55]

Bo grasped the levers of state power because it maximised his personal leverage and was the fastest way to get things done, and others followed. The world was slow to notice, at first, but the centre of Chinese politics and policies was being drawn towards Chongqing. Bo symbolised, if he did not command, a surge of Chinese state power that began to reverse the country's long and bumpy journey towards open markets, law and peaceful diplomacy with the world. Over this period of Bo's surging power, China massively increased the size and reach of its security and propaganda apparatuses, tilted the playing field against private enterprise, reversed a program to 'professionalise' the legal system and triggered fears across the region of an expansionist military power. Bo inspired hope and fear in equal measure.

Bo's game-changing political move was to recruit a city police chief from Liaoning province, Wang Lijun, who was every bit as ambitious, ruthless and calculating as he was. Wang, an ethnic Mongolian who was raised outside the usual patronage channels, showed a rare understanding of the calculating courage required to get things done in China's calcifying bureaucracy.[56]

In his old stomping grounds, Wang had been known for standing on the bonnet of his pick-up truck and firing shots into the air when he'd arrived at crime scenes, and for performing his own autopsies in order to ascertain whether 'their hearts were black or red'. He even boasted of pioneering a new technique of harvesting body organs from execution victims, while the victims were still alive. Bo brought Wang in with a leapfrog promotion to deputy police chief of Chongqing municipality in 2008, despite never having officially worked closely with him before. To all but the closest observers, it seemed a great departure from the rules of political patronage, where trust and reciprocal obligations are tested and established over long periods of time. Bo was gambling his career in Chongqing on the services of a man who had never worked directly with him.

Together, Bo and Wang purged Chongqing's entrenched power elite. Their most crucial move was to promote Wang to head of the Public Security Bureau in March 2009 and move his predecessor, Wen Qiang, to run the Justice Bureau. Investigators showed Wen's wife pictures of her husband in bed with underage prostitutes, and she promptly led them to millions of dollars wrapped in plastic and buried under their goldfish pond. Bo and Wang then moved on to Wen's sister-in-law, dubbing her 'the godmother of the Chongqing underworld' and accused her of running gambling dens, prostitution rackets and drug rings. They destroyed Wen's most important protégés. A former deputy police chief died of 'a heart attack' during interrogation, according to official media, while the chief of traffic police reportedly died after smashing his head against a wall. Bo convicted Wen Qiang in a great show trial and trumpeted news of his execution by text message. It is likely that Bo personally wrote the front-page newspaper headline: 'Wen Qiang is Dead, The People Rejoice, Chongqing is at Peace'. Bo and Wang didn't seem to care that Wen's key patron, a previous Chongqing party boss called He Guoqiang, was now the head of the Central Discipline Inspection Commission.

Running the municipal security and justice apparatus as a private army, Bo and Wang swept through the strategic heights of the bureaucracy to make it their own. Bo insisted on vetting every local newspaper report about him, sometimes delaying the news by a day in the process. He often personally vetted and edited the evening television news in a small editing office he had installed next to his office.[57] Sceptical officials soon learned to curb their tongues. A forestry official called Fang Hong posted a faeces-themed joke about 'the king of Chongqing' on the internet and then spent the following year pondering his unhelpful attitude while making Christmas decorations in a forced-labour camp.

The head of Chongqing Broadcasting Corp, Li Xiaofeng, fretted about the precipitous decline in viewers and revenue that followed Bo's demand for 'red' programming. He was gaoled, tortured, and deprived of sleep for twenty days until he delivered the confession they required. Li was 'the biggest case of official corruption in Chongqing since the founding of the People's Republic of China,' said local newspapers after Li was handed a suspended death sentence. Bo recreated a Maoist world of enemies and friends with no stable alternatives in between. 'Bo had a habit of taking on the most powerful,' Li's son-in-law told Reuters. 'He didn't kill a chicken to scare the monkeys. He killed monkeys to scare the chickens.'

Wang met almost daily with Bo, often for hours at a time, and together they sliced through the ranks of organised criminals, entrepreneurs, officials and lawyers who were in their way. 'The gangsters slashed people with knives just like butchers killing animals,' said Bo, to the enthralled and largely appreciative people of Chongqing. One entrepreneur, Chen Meirong, told how she had been bailed up by a dozen gangsters in the foyer of the Daisy Hotel in 2009 and was pressured to sign over a ¥220 million real estate development. Her daughter rescued her, but not her business. She later doused herself in petrol, lighter in hand, and tried to force her way to see the man she blamed for her ordeal – a senior official called Weng Zhenjie, who the gangsters called 'Big Brother'. The daughter was subsequently detained for nearly a year and her family didn't get its business back. And yet she thanks Bo Xilai for arresting the gangsters and cleaning up the streets. 'The police now come within three minutes when ordinary people call,' said the daughter, pointing to police cars on Chongqing's People Power Road. 'Before Bo Xilai arrived they would never come at all.'[58]

Together, Bo and Wang Lijun tore up the staid template of Chinese politics, exposing a purulent mass of corruption, violence and decadence beneath the Communist Party's shiny veneer. Bo spoke a language that neo-Maoists and nostalgic Party elders alike could understand and Wang provided the action to back it up. 'Corruption is the Party's mortal wound and degeneration of its working style is its chronic disease,' Bo said on television in December 2009, building on an old metaphor that Mao had used to begin his brutally effective 'rectification campaign' of 1942–45. 'Without help, the disease will become fatal.'

For China's growing band of courageous lawyers, activists and civil society leaders, however, Bo Xilai's Chongqing was the distilled essence of a sickness that was disabling the nation. 'Everything in China is for "interests" and nothing is for "isms",' said one such lawyer, Pu Zhiqiang, representing a fugitive Chongqing billionaire who had been stripped of all his assets. 'The power-elites use ultra-leftist methods to appropriate assets, often under the name of the environment, or justice, and once they've got them, they share among themselves in an ultra-rightist way.'

Wang Boming, publisher of the path-breaking investigative magazine *Caijing*, carefully pushed back against Bo's Chongqing Model when opportunities arose, as did his star editor, Hu Shuli, when she left to set up *Caixin* magazine. 'He's trying to mobilise society like Mao did during the Cultural Revolution, and to do that you usually have to brainwash people first,' says Wang. 'There is a legal system and he's trying to destroy it. Basically, the twenty richest guys in Chongqing – he sent them all to gaol and confiscated all their assets.'[59]

Others closer to the ground say Bo's 'red terror' took place on an even greater scale. 'The twenty richest? At least 200!' says lawyer Li Zhuang, himself a Bo victim, who has been systematically interviewing torture victims and their families. Li Zhuang's law firm, Kangda, was headed by Bo's old classmate at No. 4 Middle School, Fu Yang. 'Chongqing has thirty-eight districts and counties and the richest person in each region was arrested.' Li says billions of yuan were stripped from these entrepreneurs and absorbed into Wang's police empire. 'Those assets should [have gone to] the national treasury but instead they were "digested" at the Public Security Bureau and nobody knows how.'

Some of Wang's extra-budget income spilled into the pockets of his allies and his family, while some went into the finest facilities that any Chinese police force had ever known. He built a network of sophisticated restaurant-canteens, the centrepiece of which was a vast two-storey dining establishment with brass fittings, golden floorings and curtains at the opulent Public Security Bureau headquarters, which he renovated in downtown Chongqing. Friends fondly recall the à la carte Japanese, Chinese and Western food, followed by offerings of seasonal fruit. They say dining at the central police cafeteria was a ceremonious and austere occasion, with Wang, of course, at the centre of the liturgy. 'People wait for him before they start eating and they would often line up and applaud to welcome him into the room,' said Zhou Litai, a lawyer friend of Wang's. 'He allowed no phone calls, no casual chatting and no leftover food.' Zhou extols Wang's achievements but readily concedes his friend had something of a 'hero complex', constantly performing as if his life was a blockbuster film. Wang also built a police museum in honour of their anti-mafia campaign, which he and Bo reserved exclusively for the stream of superiors visiting from Beijing.

Bo and Wang were strategic about their targets, though, and left some of the wealthy alone. Bo carved up real estate opportunities for the businessmen he brought from Liaoning, particularly Xu Ming. He took care to protect the interests of princelings and their associates who he considered useful allies, such as the nephew of a powerful former national security chief who dominated the city's logistics sector. Alongside Xu Ming, arguably the biggest financial beneficiary of Bo's administrative discretion was, ironically, Weng Zhenjie, the man who some call 'the Godfather of Chongqing'.

Weng Zhenjie had leveraged connections in China's military-industrial complex to work his way to the heart of the city's state-run financial system, while simultaneously controlling underground financiers and debt collectors. He hired one of former president Jiang's nieces to sit on the board of his infrastructure firm and forged links with other important political and military families. Local entrepreneurs soon learnt to cooperate and share their commercial opportunities – or risk losing them.

Bringing down Weng would have opened up his vast financial resources, earned Wang Lijun even greater glory and authority and also damaged Weng's closest senior associate: the one man who competed with him for Bo's attention, the Chongqing mayor, Huang Qifan. Bo blocked Wang's path because it would have been politically destabilising. Late in 2010, Wang quietly approached a disgruntled entrepreneur, Zhang Mingyu, with a clandestine agenda. 'Wang wanted to get rid of Weng and asked me to report him,' says Zhang, whose testimony gives credence to those who argue Bo controlled the Chongqing mafia by making it his own.

Zhang had played endless hands of poker at Weng Zhenjie's expansive villa – where each player was accompanied by an attractive woman – and took care to lose at a ratio of ten to one. His two million yuan in gambling debts were promptly paid, his modest winnings never collected. Twice he rushed to answer random demands to deliver a total of ¥1.35 million in cash to Weng's villa door. Zhang thought he knew the unwritten rules ('I call it the balance of terror – you do bad by me, I expose you'), but it turned out that Weng knew the game much better. When the courtship was complete, Weng's thugs cornered Zhang in a park and beat him up, drove him out of town, and Weng took possession of Zhang's two billion yuan real estate portfolio.[60]

In January 2011, on the steps of the city's annual meeting of the National People's Congress, Zhang presented a dossier of Weng's alleged crimes to the Chongqing mayor and broadcast the contents over the internet. One congress delegate dumping criminal allegations on another was unheard of anywhere in China, let alone in Bo's Chongqing. It triggered a furore and attracted interest from investigators in Beijing, as Wang Lijun had intended. But Weng seemed entirely unfazed. 'I believe that innocence is self-apparent,' said Weng, responding to the allegations in an interview with an obscure Guangdong paper. 'I have been reading some history books recently, and the protagonists of history always meet the resistance of the little people, and always the result is that the evil-doers kill themselves.' Weng, like Bo, had grown up steeped in the history of emperors from Qin Shihuang to Mao Zedong. In this world, innocence is a quality of the powerful while the weak, guilty or not, commit suicide. Weng was confident that Bo Xilai has assessed the balance of power, as he had, and would not extend his mafia crackdown up to the edge of China's princeling-led military-industrial complex.

Wang lost interest in pursing Weng around the time Weng established a ¥150 million 'police compensation fund' for officers injured in the anti-mafia campaign, to be administered by Wang personally. Wang allowed Weng's hybrid state-private trust company to become a repository for seized assets, including, apparently, the Hilton Hotel. Weng knew he was safe when Wang Lijun finally invited him for dinner in his palatial police cafeteria.

Mostly, however, the unseemly details remained concealed from view, as Bo became the pin-up boy for the new left, the old left, the Maoist left and, it appeared, anyone who was attracted to the allure of shiny rising power. Chinese and US-educated professors filled pages of newsprint explaining the genius of Bo's Chongqing Model. 'Chongqing represents a new economic pattern that transcends left and right,' said Tsinghua University's Professor Cui Zhiyuan, a Chicago University-educated leader of the New Left movement. Cui claimed Bo had simultaneously nurtured the private sector and massively expanded the state sector and created a new template of participatory politics. 'Chongqing is an experiment to promote more political democracy for the common people,' he added, before acknowledging that he had been on the Chongqing government payroll.[61]

Bo went to huge lengths to demonstrate support

from powerful people, or at least the appearance of it. President Hu Jintao's brother, Deng Xiaoping's brother and even Henry Kissinger made high-profile pilgrimages to Chongqing. 'I saw the vision for the future,' said Henry Kissinger after addressing a mass red-singing performance in June 2011. 'I am shaken by the vitality of the city.' In a remarkable departure from China's Beijing-centric conventions, most members of the Politburo Standing Committee travelled to Chongqing and were reported in the state-run media as showing effusive support.

Despite their families' tangled history, and whatever his personal views, Vice-President Xi Jinping shared the same political patron as Bo Xilai, in former president Jiang Zemin. And he encouraged and benefited from Bo raising the prestige of the old revolutionaries. As soon as Xi was firmly anointed as President Hu's successor, after receiving a key military appointment late in 2010, he flew to Chongqing to tell Bo that his 'singing red' campaign had 'gone deeply into the hearts of the people and was worthy of praise'. Xi's lavish endorsement filled the full front page of the *Chongqing Daily* and ran for twenty minutes on the local evening news.

Pointedly, though, President Hu Jintao and Premier Wen Jiabao both stayed away.

Spectre of the
Cultural Revolution

The Red Guard generation that is running China today had signed on to the promise of utopia in the 1960s only to see it crumble before their eyes. Among them was Yang Fan, professor of economics at China University of Political Science and Law, who was actively involved in the 'rebel' Red Guards who opposed the initial princeling Red Guards at No. 4 Middle School. Yang was a classmate of Bo's boisterous younger brother, Bo Xicheng, and stayed close to the Bo family despite being on the other side of the princeling divide. After the Bo's were 'struck down', and the tide had turned against the red aristocracy more generally, Yang personally arrested the key princeling rival of Bo's elder brother, who had beaten him to lead the school's Cultural Revolution Group.[62] In 2002, Yang co-founded the leftist internet phenomenon *Utopia*, which became the most important cheerleading platform for Bo's ascendancy and also led relentless assaults against Bo's leadership rivals – particularly Premier Wen Jiabao. Early in 2011, Yang co-authored a laudatory book called *The Chongqing Model*, which applauded Bo's attack on entrenched privilege.

In the northern spring of 2011, however, even Professor Yang was reversing course. 'His program should include democracy, rule of law, market economics, but now it is too close to the Old Left and New Left and the Cultural Revolution,' said Yang. He recited a seven-character Chinese aphorism, about how a daughter-in-law suffers for years at the hands of her mother-in-law before becoming one herself. 'Maybe Bo has this psychology and is becoming a mini-Mao,' said Yang. 'Bo's problems in Chongqing will be exposed and it will turn to chaos.'

The case that drove the leftist economist and family friend to change his mind on Bo's Chongqing Model, and which galvanised Chinese civil society in a way that had previously seemed impossible given the political constraints, was the eighteen-month odyssey of a courageous and well-regarded lawyer, Li Zhuang. Li's primary offence was probably that he had entertained the idea of defending Wen Qiang, Wang Lijun's predecessor as police chief, who was

Bo and Wang's number-one target in their bid to clean out the local power structure. 'Wen's family contacted me through a good friend of mine in the Beijing armed police,' says Li, adding that the engagement did not work out. Li did, however, robustly defend one of Wen's alleged mafia henchmen, Gong Gangmo, who had accumulated a multi-billion yuan fortune by manufacturing a share of the nine million motorbikes that Chongqing makes each year. Not only was Gong facing the red terror of Chongqing justice, but his wife was on her death bed with cancer. 'Gong's brother knelt down in front of me at the second floor of Liang'an Cafe,' says Li, referring to a popular Chongqing meeting spot. 'So I felt a sense of compassion and couldn't turn him down.'

Li Zhuang believes the alleged gangster Gong Gangmo was indeed guilty of bribing Wen Qiang, even if that was par for the course in a country where security officials tend to run the unsavoury establishments where business deals are done. Gong also kept a diamond-encrusted Browning gun under the cushions of his sofa, a prestigious gift he'd received but never sought to use. He had no connection, however, to the underworld gangsters – with their ten kilograms of drugs, seventeen guns and four murders – who he was accused of leading, says Li. When Gong appeared in court he recanted an earlier confession and said it was extracted by torture. That was not a claim made lightly, given the treatment typically meted out to uncooperative suspects in Bo and Wang's Chongqing justice system. 'Twice he tried to kill himself by hitting his head against the wall, and he then tried to bite off his own tongue,' said another lawyer, describing the ordeal of Gong's co-accused, who was executed after confessing to the charges against him. 'Guards ripped off his partially severed tongue but did not allow him medical treatment for a further two days.'[63]

Bo Xilai and Wang Lijun were not accustomed to facing defendants who did not plead guilty. It went against the logic of the revolution, where suspects were necessarily guilty or else the Party would not have accused them. It also set an unhelpful precedent. So they traced Gong's lawyer, Li Zhuang, by the signal of his phone, and abducted him from the outskirts of Beijing. Wang, forever the actor in his own screenplay, was waiting for him at Chongqing airport. Backlit by the flashing lights of dozens of police cars, he said: 'Li Zhuang, we meet again!'

When it was Li's turn to appear in a Chongqing court, on the charge of coaching his client to falsely testify, he recanted his own statement, just as his client had done: 'My confession is fake!' Li's own defence lawyer adroitly spread the news and the

Chinese internet lit up.

Scholars debated how the far left had converged with the extreme right in the city they sometimes referred to as 'Tomato' to get around internet censors (the Chinese characters sound the same as 'Red City in the West'). They explored the shared roots of communism, Maoism and fascism, where law was subordinate to the needs of the Party-state and the state defined as the ultimate expression of the people. They recalled how Hitler had also rallied the masses to dispossess the entrepreneurial class – which in Germany was the Jews. 'Statist thinking is gaining ground in the mainstream ideology of officialdom, and may even be practiced on a large scale in some regions through "singing Red songs and striking hard at crime",' wrote one of China's leading historians, Xu Jilin, in a paper he was invited to deliver at a closed-door seminar organised by leading serving and retired financial officials in early 2011. 'The history of Germany and Japan in the 1930s shows that if statism fulfils its potential, it will lead the entire nation into catastrophe.'

Professor Xu charted how China's New Left – Bo's intellectual support base – had flipped from criticising the 'neo-liberal' Communist Party of the early 1990s to cheerleading its contemporary muscular incarnation. He called it the 'collective swing to the right on the part of the radical left'. He was echoing a fateful warning from Bo Yibo at the start of the Cultural Revolution: 'To be a leftist among the leftists is to be a leftist in quotation marks, which is also to be a rightist'.

Fourteen months after Li Zhuang's arrest, Bo and Wang laid fresh trumped-up charges against him, just months prior to his scheduled release. They wanted to prevent the risk that Li might cause trouble ahead of the 18th Party Congress. Instead, they ignited a furore. In January 2011, Zhang Mingyu's public dossier on the city's protected godfather, Weng Zhenjie, had exposed a hairline crack in Bo's Chongqing bastion, and now Li Zhuang's courageous defence of his client and then himself opened it wider. Bo's Chongqing Model became a proxy battlefield for raging debates about China's future. China's long-suffering but determined band of liberal lawyers and intellectuals took the invitation to challenge the tyranny they believed Bo stood for. Bo's abuse of his justice system become a bigger story than his success in putting mobsters away.

The man who triggered the public uproar over Li Zhuang's re-arrest in March 2011 was the lawyer who had previously represented him, Chen Youxi. Chen, an exceptionally sharp, courageous and demonstrative advocate, explained on his *weibo* microblog – a Chinese variant of Twitter with 250 million users – what it was like to appear in a court controlled by Bo Xilai and Wang Lijun. He exposed how Li Zhuang had initially 'confessed' in circumstances where a fellow accused had 'committed suicide' in a nearby crowded cell in broad daylight. He said lawyers in Chongqing were reduced to actors on Bo's stage. The better their defence, he wrote, the more convincing the theatre.

Chen launched a fusillade of fiery essays, which were pushed along by netizens and liberal-minded media publishers faster than censors could delete them. He raised the spectre of the return of the Cultural Revolution and not just in Bo's Chongqing. 'During the Cultural Revolution there was nothing left of the law, and this caused the entire nation to slide into civil strife,' wrote Chen, in the *Southern Weekend* newspaper. 'Injustice prevailed everywhere, and even the chairman of the republic [Liu Shaoqi] could not be protected.' Only when China's laws were applied to officials as well as ordinary people could 'every person be free of fear'. Unbeknown to the public, the debate raging around Bo's abuse of his legal apparatus penetrated deep into officialdom. Untainted information could not penetrate through China's stratified and calcified bureaucracy, so it was relayed from civil society to

Beijing via princeling channels.

Chen Youxi, Li Zhuang's lawyer, sent his writings and dossiers to every supervisory body and potentially sympathetic powerful person he could think of. One person who requested a meeting was Hu Deping, eldest son of the popular reformist leader Hu Yaobang, whom Bo Yibo had purged in 1987 and Xi Jinping's father had defended. Chen's warnings about a return of the Cultural Revolution dovetailed with what the Hu family had been privately warning about for three decades. Hu held meetings with some of his father's protégés in the leadership, including President Hu Jintao, according to sources close to those conversations. He then moved to forge an anti-Bo consensus among many of China's marginalised and liberal-leaning princelings. 'In recent years, for whatever reason, there seems to be a "revival" of something like advocating the Cultural Revolution,' said Hu Deping, at a seminar he hosted in August 2011. 'Some people cherish it; some do not believe in the Cultural Revolution but nevertheless exploit it and play it up. I think we must guard this bottom line!' Presciently, he honed in on the need to forge mechanisms to mediate the power games between party leaders and foreshadowed the ructions that are now taking place: 'If we really want to carry out democratization of inner-party political life, the cost is going to be enormous. Do we have the courage to accept that cost? If we do it now, there is a cost certainly. Do we dare to bear the cost? Is now the right time? I cannot say for sure. However, I think it might create some "chaos" in some localities, some temporary "chaos", and some localised "chaos". We should be prepared.'

A second princeling channel for transmitting information involved the lawyer who started it all, Li Zhuang. The law firm he was working for was founded and headed by another prestigious liberal princeling, Fu Yang, who was the student leader of Bo Xilai's class at No. 4 Middle School. Fu's father, Peng Zhen, was one of the Eight Immortals and even more senior than Bo Yibo. The fathers fought together in northwest China and both lived well into their nineties. Fu Yang's father happened to be the Party's leading legal expert for the first four decades of the People's Republic. His expertise, ironically, stemmed from a handful of law books he was given to read in the 1930s when he was imprisoned in a Kuomintang gaol. The power of Fu Yang's inherited prestige and connections made his law firm uniquely capable of defending fallen officials and businessmen, such as those allegedly working with Chongqing's former police chief, Wen Qiang. Bo and Wang saw the law firm's involvement as a dangerous provocation, if not a political conspiracy. Shortly after arresting Li Zhuang, they hinted at the bigger background game in an article planted in the *China Youth Daily*: 'As Li Zhuang arrived at Chongqing, he began to play the peacock, saying many times, "Do you know my background? Do you know who my boss is?"'[64]

Fu Yang, the law firm boss and son of Peng Zhen, had been humiliated alongside Bo Xilai during the schoolyard criticism sessions at No. 4. In the early 1980s, they remained so close that Bo sought his advice in dealing with proceedings against his first wife, who refused to divorce him. Their politics drifted apart, however, as Fu's family came to talk about rule of law and Bo's family locked into a more conservative stance. Fu Yang takes great pride that his father is officially credited with developing China's legal system. He exonerates Bo from persistent myths about his supposed brutality during the Cultural Revolution but he cannot forgive his old schoolmate for desecrating his father's legacy.

'My father participated in and presided over the building of the legal system of New China, leaving aside the Cultural Revolution period,' said Fu Yang, speaking in the boardroom of his Beijing law firm. 'When the Cultural Revolution was over, when he was leading the National People's Congress, he attached great importance to the fact that the legal system had been completely destroyed during the Cultural Revolution and that people's rights, particularly human rights, were trampled underfoot. After he passed away, he was given the title as the "key founder of China's socialist legal system". I absolutely adopted my father's fundamental understanding of law including the tenet that "everyone is equal before the law".'

Fu Yang rejects the popular teleological view that Bo had nurtured an evil side since his Red Guard days at school. 'I can't connect anything from Bo's days in school and in the Cultural Revolution to what took place in Chongqing,' says Fu. Instead, he believes Bo became consumed by his own power because the system allowed him to. 'In my view, the only explanation is that he massively expanded his ambitions. His personality changed when his position changed, and it resulted in his abusing power and disregarding law.'

Fu Yang had steered clear of active politics from the time Deng Xiaoping's eldest son, Deng Pufang, had set him up with his own independent law firm in the late 1980s. But Bo Xilai's double-arrest of one of his star lawyers, Li Zhuang, forced him to re-engage. Not only had his former classmate thrown one of his most talented lawyers in gaol on fabricated charges, he had made a mockery of his father's legal system. 'Of course it damaged the legal system,' said Fu. 'I don't know what Bo Xilai was thinking . . .'

Fu was guarded and lawyer-like in his first interview with a foreigner, but did not dispute claims by close friends that Li Zhuang's arrest had made him apoplectic. Fu, who enjoys getting together with friends with a bottle of *moutai* – the potent Chinese white spirit – confirmed his sister was so nervous about what he might say or do that might escalate their feud that she ordered him not to drink outside his own home for six weeks after Li Zhuang's arrest. 'She knew Bo was capable of anything,' said a close family friend.

Divining the actions and inclinations of top-level leaders is a hazardous pastime, given the impenetrability of the Chinese system. Fu Yang says he refrained from harnessing his political capital and lobbying top leaders directly. Many believe, however, that his old patron Deng Pufang – the reclusive son of Deng Xiaoping who has been wheelchair-bound since being thrown from a third floor window during the Cultural Revolution, and who had bequeathed to Fu his law firm – had had a quiet but decisive word to President Hu Jintao about excesses in Chongqing and the importance of the rule of law. If so, then President Hu Jintao was being simultaneously urged to act by the eldest sons of Hu Yaobang and Deng Xiaoping, the two men most responsible for raising him from obscurity to president of China. Bo Xilai's momentum had been stalled.

According to several lawyers and princelings close to the case, in April 2011 President Hu 'expressed an opinion' that Li Zhuang should be released. Senior legal sources confirm that such a message was passed down to them by both the Supreme People's Court and Procuratorate. On 22 April, seeing the array of forces against him, Bo Xilai dropped the second batch of charges against Li Zhuang. It was one of the few back downs in Bo's thirty-year career.

The bad blood between Bo Xilai, the maverick princeling, and China's two most prominent central leaders, Hu Jintao and Wen Jiabao, went back at least a generation.[65] Hu and Wen were both born to ordinary families. They had bucked the odds by proving competent in their jobs and securing crucial patrons at each step of their careers. Wen's family had been persecuted by the princeling Red Guards early in the Cultural Revolution, in Tianjin. Later, it was the ordinary-born Red Guards from his university who arrested Bo's father in 1966 and began his persecution. Hu Jintao's father, a tea merchant, was persecuted during the Cultural Revolution and never rehabilitated, although the details have been assiduously buried. In the 1980s, Bo's father had led the internal assault on Hu and Wen's most important patron, the reformist leader Hu Yaobang.

More recently, Premier Wen's lonely advocacy for democracy and the rule of law had been colliding with Bo's nebulous neo-Maoist predilections. In 2010 and 2011, Wen and Bo had major confrontations in the Politburo including over Wen's advocacy for political reform. It is impossible to know the extent to which Bo's patronage ties to Jiang Zemin emboldened him to challenge the Hu-Wen Administration, but close Jiang associates say the former president took Bo's side. 'Bo will do anything to anyone, except the Jiang family, and Jiang's support for him has never wavered,' said the Chinese head of an international investment bank – whose job requires him to immerse himself in the hidden webs of power and patronage among China's leading families. Speaking well before Bo's fall, the investment banker said Jiang had told Bo to confront Wen on his advocacy of political reform in the Politburo. 'Jiang wants Bo for the security job,' he added, referring to the powerful job occupied by another Jiang protégé, Zhou Yongkang, who was due to retire from the Politburo Standing Committee at the 18th Party Congress.[66] A princeling friend of the Jiang family, who had recently retired from a minister-level job but remains intimately involved in China's ideological debates, put it this way: 'Whatever Wen advocated, Jiang opposed.'[67]

In a factionally divided Politburo, Hu and Wen could not afford to confront a powerfully connected princeling like Bo Xilai directly, as much as they were growing to fear and despise him. But, if they took great care, they could undermine him from below.

Murder on the Yangtze

Investigators sent from the Central Commission for Discipline Inspection appeared at the old stomping grounds of Bo's police chief, Wang Lijun in the northern spring of 2011, at about the same time as Bo and Wang dropped the charges against Li Zhuang. The Commission is feared for its powers but known more for its own corruption and dysfunction than its achievements. It is headed by He Guoqiang, a Politburo Standing Committee member whose family is notorious for inside business dealings, and whose protégé, Wen Qiang, had just been executed in Chongqing. Important Party leaders each have a loyalist within the commission, minimising the risk that the networks of individual leaders will be undermined by an unexpected investigation. The Commission cannot open a formal high-level investigation without sign-off from the Politburo Standing Committee. However, there are two senior Commission officials – an ageing warrior called He Yong and 'Iron Lady' Ma Wen – who are known to be tough and wily adversaries.

The year had begun with Wang Lijun secretly encouraging an entrepreneur to dump a public dossier on the businessman-official-gangland leader, Weng Zhenjie. He Yong, known for his loyalty to President Hu Jintao inside the discipline commission, signed a related investigation but it didn't get off the ground, according to a participant in that endeavour.

In Tieling city, Liaoning province, where Wang Lijun had been police chief a decade earlier, his successor as police chief was secretly detained in May, 2011.[68] Later that month Bo made a show of faith by promoting Wang to deputy mayor in Chongqing.

In August, Premier Wen Jiabao's personal delegate at the discipline commission, a fellow native from Tianjin, Ma Wen, appeared in Chongqing. She made a phone call to President Hu Jintao in Beijing from a state guesthouse that was later ascertained to have been bugged by officials in Chongqing, prompting another avenue of investigation.[69] On 21 September, the former deputy mayor of Tieling was found dead in a river in nearby Shenyang, which police attributed to suicide.[70] Unconfirmed rumours say Wang may have secretly met central discipline inspection officials in Beijing that month, hoping to strike a deal. Bo himself was known to be unbreakable but, with enough pressure, perhaps his circle could be broken at its weakest links.

Just as Bo and Wang did whatever it took to advance their personal ambitions, in a system that had no institutional checks or balances, so too did Bo's petite, glamorous and formidable wife. They had all grown up in a world where winners took everything and those who were not constantly accumulating power lived in constant fear of having it stripped away. Gu Kailai held no official position but she lived at the court of an emperor and became a central player in his machine. She and Bo appeared to grow emotionally distant as he became consumed by work and liaised with younger women, according to several friends, but he also trusted her, appreciated her as the mother of his son, and used her to bypass the cumbersome Party apparatus and secure the family's political and personal interests. Gu 'possessed a wealth of knowledge about cultures around the world,' said Bo, at the 2010 National People's Congress. 'Her knowledge, especially her legal background, was very helpful in the efforts to crack down on organised crime.' Their arrangement was not unlike that of Mao and his wife, Jiang Qing, albeit on a much smaller scale.

Gu, however, had become increasingly withdrawn, fragile and unpredictable as Bo rose closer to the summit of power, and they became a more prominent potential target for those they offended. She continued to lose weight, she was constantly exhausted and occasionally fainted.

After Gu shelved her own professional aspirations, their son, Bo Guagua, hinted at her depression and sympathised with her frustrations. 'Dad often talks to me about Mom, he thinks she is great, very thoughtful, very creative, whatever she does she does well,' Bo Guagua said in a 2009 interview with the *Chengdu Evening News*, later expunged from its website.[71] 'Since stepping down she's been living like a hermit and doesn't attend any social events; when Dad wants her to come to events she won't. I can understand; she is most unwilling to be in Dad's shadow, and lose herself. Right now she reads all day.'

In subsequent court proceedings, Xinhua News Agency said she was being treated for chronic insomnia, anxiety, depression and paranoia. 'She used to take anxiolytics, antidepressants and sedative hypnotic drugs, and she also received combined treatment by taking antipsychotic drugs, but the curative effect was not enduring,' said Xinhua. 'She developed a certain degree of physical and psychological dependence on sedative hypnotic drugs, which resulted in mental disorders.'

None of the accounts canvassed by the court, media or blogosphere, however, get close to the family's private understanding of what was going on. In 2006, in Beijing, Western- and Chinese-trained doctors had tried but failed to get to diagnose her fragile physical and mental state. This is when the family, in desperation, was introduced to a legendary small-town cop – whose name was Wang Lijun. Wang's investigation led to Gu's medicine cabinet. He found that the yellow powder in the capsules containing her daily dose of *congcao* – an ultra-expensive organism only found on the Tibetan plateau, which behaves like a worm in winter and sprouts like grass in the spring – had been replaced with a darker tinged powder that contained traces of mercury. The small dosages, taken over a long period of time, sapped her strength and her sanity and, eventually, made her critically ill. Two close family aides were sacked in relation to the adulterated tablets, according to family sources, and in one great bound Wang had won his way into the inner court. Wang followed Bo to Chongqing in 2008, where he was quickly promoted to police chief.

—

Despite Gu's growing instability, many of Bo's most important officials and associates readily took their cues from her, including his police chief Wang Lijun. 'I visited Bogu Kailai's home often, and I thought she treated me quite well,' said Wang. [72] Many Chongqing officials, including Wang's deputy police chief, owed their allegiance primarily to Gu. In 2008, Gu hired her father's young and steadfastly loyal bodyguard, Zhang Xiaojun, and brought him into Gu's inner circle. His primary task was to liaise with and protect Gu's overseas son, Bo Guagua, while on the payroll of the Chongqing Party's General Office. The unbridled administrative power enjoyed by the Bo family's lieutenants, and the absence of accountability, proved to be a lucrative combination. Xu Ming, Bo's favoured businessman who followed him from Dalian, was the most important financial gatekeeper. In 2010, for example, Wang released three people from gaol after Xu funnelled him a ¥2.85 million bribe, in the form of two apartments signed over to a relative in Beijing. Similarly, another Bo crony called Yu Junshi, the former PLA intelligence officer, made payments of ¥200 000 for Wang to release a detainee.[73] Justice in Chongqing was a commodity that could be bought and sold – except where the Bo family's personal and political interests were at stake.

Gu's actions grew more extreme and unpredictable

as the stakes grew higher and the family's enemies circled in Beijing. There was persistent but unsubstantiated talk that her affairs had been probed by investigators. Tensions arose between Wang and Gu as Beijing investigators turned up the heat on Wang. Wang describes an incident on 12 August 2011, where Bo Guagua phoned and wanted to see him but Wang lied to say he was three hours away, at the far end of the municipality. Whatever Bo Guagua wanted to talk about it was evidently urgent, as he drove to find him and nearly had a traffic accident along the way. His mother, Gu Kailai, was furious at Wang.[74]

Lurking deeper in the family's vault of dynastic secrets was Gu's conviction that the family of Bo's first wife envied her so much that they would physically try to harm her family. It didn't ease her paranoia that Bo's son from his first marriage, Li Wangzhi, sometimes known as Brendan Li, had long dropped the Bo family name and never forgave his father for abandoning them. Sometime around the turn of the millennium, Li was brought back into the family, but then cast out again in about 2006. The fact of the bitter feud is not disputed but the cause is heavily contested. On one side, Li is accused of trading on his father's name, without Bo's knowledge, to the extent that he would take business associates to the patriarch Bo Yibo's vacant home in Zhongnahai in order to give a misleading impression that he was the favoured son. Li Wangzhi's father-in-law's pharmaceutical company, Dalian Zhen Ao He Sun, had been hugely profitable, at least since Bo Yibo had publicly bestowed a couplet of his calligraphy upon it. In one version of the contested facts, however, Li obtained a crucial licence – the first licence to direct-sell pharmaceutical products – from Bo's Ministry of Commerce in 2006, without Bo's knowledge. Media reports show that the licence was soon stripped away. Earlier, Li had prospered as an investment banker for Citi, while his father worked in Dalian, but struggled when he could not easily demonstrate his father's favour. Macquarie Group, the Australian investment bank, later invited him on board to open doors but found that investors didn't treat him as a genuine princeling. 'The problem was that nobody knew who he was,' said a Macquarie executive.[75]

Li named his own company after a duke in the seventh century BC from the Bo family's ancestral home, who fled into exile because his father made his half-brother the crown prince. The duke fought back and regained the crown.[76] He had also adopted the alias Li Xiaobai, after another spurned seventh-century BC prince who won back his crown. Gu came to fear that such fantasies might come true.

In fact, Wang Lijun's detective work suggested that she had good reason to feel afraid. Wang obtained confessions from Gu's driver and another family aide, who admitted that they had been bribed to tamper with Gu's Tibetan caterpillar grass powder. A lawyer for the family said the alleged attack left Gu with permanent health problems, including shaking hands. She has rarely been seen in public since. Wang's stunning findings were never used in a prosecution, but he had earned the trust and gratitude and a place at the family court.[77]

Bo and Gu acted as if their family were constantly under siege. In October 2011, the month before Heywood's murder, Bo summoned to Chongqing a man named Li Xiaoxue, who occupied a crucial position in the stock exchange regulatory authority. In the incestuous world of the communist aristocracy, Li was the brother of Li Danyu, Bo's first wife, and he was married to a sister of Gu Kailai. Bo pointed to a stack of papers – Wang Lijun's forensic report – detailing a plot by Li Wangzhi to poison Gu. Bo wanted to know which side of the family his brother-in-law would choose. Li's family confirm the fact of the feud and the nature of the allegations, but categorically deny that they are true.

Into this crucible of clan, state and ancient dynastic courtroom politics – where there were virtually no boundaries between the affairs of Chongqing municipality and those of its leading family – walked the well-spoken, impeccably mannered, small-time English businessman, Neil Heywood.

Born in 1970, Heywood was a quietly charming, chain-smoking adventurer who carried a slightly contrived air of mystery. He wore beige linen suits through the northern Chinese summer and tawny corduroy trousers with a Barbour hunting jacket when the weather turned cool. He lived for films, particularly spy films, and drove a maroon S-Type Jaguar around the crowded Beijing streets. Heywood had been schooled at Harrow and studied international relations at Warwick University. In the early nineties he left behind the rarefied upper middle class of London to see the world. He landed in Beijing and mastered the language. According to Heywood's friends, he headed for Dalian and sprayed dozens of introduction letters to local officials, until one of them, Bo Xilai, replied. It was in Dalian that Heywood met his future wife, Wang Lulu.

It has been widely reported that Heywood's fortunes soared because he took on a mentor role for Bo Guagua and helped smooth his passage into Harrow, the boyhood stomping ground of Lord Byron and Winston Churchill. 'Where better to get the boy schooled than Neil's alma mater, Harrow –

that bastion of the establishment and route into the Old Boy's network which has so many parallels with Chinese webs of influence and patronage,' said one of Heywood's acquaintances, Tom Reed, writing in *The Times*. 'Neil got his sponsor while Bo got his son an urbane and charming guide to the obscure rituals of English society.'[78] Gu Kailai, however, contradicted such accounts by telling the court that they did not meet until Guagua was already ensconced at Harrow. 'It was about 2005, when my son was studying in Britain, that Neil Heywood wrote us a letter of introduction.'

Heywood's fortunes seemed to peak around the time the Bo family moved to Chongqing, especially after Gu fell out with the man who had been her primary conduit to the Western world, the French architect Patrick Devillers.

However and whenever they became acquainted, it is clear that Heywood was thrilled to be drawn into the 'inner circle' of a family that ruled one of the world's fastest growing regional economies like a private fiefdom. 'Neil recalled, years later, flying into Chongqing with Bo the night he took charge of the province in November 2007,' wrote Reed. 'The sprawling metropolis looked like *Sin City*, the 2005 Robert Rodriguez movie about vigilante justice, Bo observed.' Some who knew Heywood suggest he was not averse to embellishing his stories.

Heywood worked occasionally with a close Chinese friend at Aston Martin, providing the British car-dealing establishment with the demeanour and appearance that was needed to support the brand favoured by James Bond. He performed due diligence work, requiring him to burrow into the murky world of Chinese companies and relationships, sometimes on behalf of a firm called Hakluyt, founded by former secret intelligence officials at MI6. He liaised occasionally with the British embassy, giving them snippets of insight into the workings of China's rising political star, Bo Xilai. Officials insist the casual relationship with Her Majesty's Government was nothing more than that, although China's ever-paranoid counter-espionage officers are unlikely to have been so sanguine. In November, the *Wall Street Journal* reported Heywood had actually become a casual informant for an officer of MI6, the British intelligence agency, supplying information about the Bos. Below the Union Jack bumper sticker on Heywood's Jaguar was a number plate that included the digits '007', a code that he would become known by on the Chinese internet when 'Heywood' was banned as a search term.

The details of Heywood's relationship with the Bo family remains encased within China's opaque and politicised judicial system, the closed world of British establishment business dealings and Heywood's scared and protective family. Individual motives are further obscured by multiple agendas and what appears to be a disinformation campaign by some close to the Bo family. It seems clear, however, that Heywood knew too much. The fact that Heywood was even perceived to be privy to sensitive information made him a weak link in the Bo family chain.

Gu came to believe she had been 'betrayed' by someone in 'the inner circle' just as her husband was making his stand for national leadership. One friend told the *Wall Street Journal* that Gu had demanded a pledge of loyalty and had even insisted that members of the inner circle divorce their wives. Whatever Gu's private motivations, no one in Chongqing – from her powerful husband down – appears to have tried to rein her in. Heywood fell out with Gu around 2010, as she battled drugs and depression, although he still kept in touch with Bo Guagua. Heywood's friends say Gu's deepening paranoia made him fearful for his own safety. Those fears, it seems, were outweighed by his desperation to repair the only prestigious and potentially lucrative Chinese relationship he had.

Heywood lived comfortably with his wife and children in a leafy gated compound in Beijing's main expatriate district, not far from the airport.

Their eleven-year-old daughter and seven-year-old son were attending a nearby international school. While internal reports of the Party's preliminary investigations suggested he was a conduit for the Bo family sending millions of yuan overseas, no evidence has come to light to support those suggestions. Associates of Heywood say they never saw any hint that he handled large sums of money. Subsequent Chinese court proceedings describe him acting on behalf of investors in a vast real estate development project in Chongqing, and a more modest one in France, both of which flowed from Gu introducing Heywood to the businessman Xu Ming, but neither of which got off the ground. 'She introduced him to serve as a proxy to a company and participate in the planning of a land project,' says the court account, by the Xinhua News Agency.[79]

The court's account of Gu's written testimony claims Heywood went so far as to detain Bo Guagua in a room in England, although the nature and timing of these allegations are at best obscure. An email exchange presented in court suggests the Englishman presented Bo Guagua, scion of the red aristocracy, with some sort of extortion deal to receive $20 million in lieu of ten per cent of expected profits from the failed property developments. It said Bo Guagua agreed that his family should accept partial responsibility for Heywood's foregone earnings. On 10 November, Heywood told Bo Guagua he 'will be destroyed' unless he paid the money, according to the Chinese translation of the email read out in court. 'To me, that was more than a threat,' Gu said in her written testimony. 'I must fight to my death to stop the craziness of Neil Heywood.' The court account of Heywood's alleged threats is vague and incomplete and considered by many to be implausible. They have also been contested by Bo Guagua.

Two days after this alleged email correspondence, Heywood received an unexpected phone call from Bo Guagua's liaison, Zhang Xiaojun. Heywood returned Zhang's call half an hour later and accepted his fateful invitation. On 13 November, a Sunday, Zhang met Heywood in Beijing, at Gu's request, and escorted him by plane to Chongqing. Gu had been preparing for the meeting by getting a local Communist Party official to shop around for a potion that contained cyanide. They settled on a poison for exterminating rats and dogs called Three Steps – Drop.[80]

Heywood was driven to the three-star Lucky Holiday Hotel – a Gu favourite –perched on a high ridge in the leafy Southern Hills, across the Yangtze River south of Chongqing city, at the very end of the road. The interiors are gloomy, with mould in the crevices and paint peeling off the walls, but the gardens are lush and landscaped. Gu took Heywood to dinner. Perhaps she attempted to ease his anxious mind. Afterwards, Heywood walked up towards the No. 16 villa, where a room had been prepared for him. On either side of the concrete path are large overhanging trees, their shapes and shadows accentuated by spotlights, while classical elevator musical emanates from speakers concealed within the camellias and azaleas beneath. From the living room of his villa he could take in the spectacular neon skyline of the Chongqing CBD, framed by dark valley ridges on either side and reflected on the Yangtze River in the foreground. He retired to his room, No. 5.

Gu gave Zhang a glass bottle and told him, for the first time, her objective. At nine o'clock she knocked on Heywood's door and entered with a bottle of Royal Salute whisky and Chinese tea. Zhang and two other retainers waited outside.

Heywood, a near-teetotaller, was soon struggling to hold his alcohol, according to written testimony presented in court. Gu phoned for Zhang. He entered as Heywood vomited, over Zhang's shirt, and fell on the bathroom floor. Zhang handed Gu the poison cocktail, in the glass bottle, and dragged Heywood onto his bed. Heywood asked for water, and Gu obliged. She poured the cyanide compound into a small soy sauce bottle, mixed it with water and strode to the side of his bed. According to the Xinhua account of Zhang's court testimony, 'She dripped the toxic mixture into Heywood's mouth as she was talking to him.'

Gu scattered drug capsules on the hotel floor in a half-hearted effort to make the death look self-inflicted. When they could no longer make out his pulse, she hung the 'Do Not Disturb' sign and told a waiter that Heywood was drunk and should be left alone. Security cameras showed Gu, Zhang and the two retainers leaving the scene at 11.38 p.m. Beyond the mechanical, matter-of-fact manner in which Gu murdered a friend, it is striking how utterly uncon-cerned she seemed that she might possibly be caught. Instead of fleeing the vicinity, Gu simply retired to her own villa, No. 3.[81] All the staff at Lucky Holiday Hotel have since been replaced and instructed not to talk. The buildings have been re-numbered, with the result that both Gu's No. 3 and Heywood's No. 16 have been erased from the map.

Throughout these extraordinary events, Gu treated the Chongqing government as an extension of the family political enterprise. Her husband's most senior officials played their assigned roles as loyal courtiers even when it meant being accessories to murder. Gu was justified in being nervous about the forces that were aligning against her husband in Beijing. She was also right to be anxious about the loyalty of the 'inner circle'. She should, however, have been focusing her suspicions closer to home.

The immediate circumstances leading up to Heywood's death are clouded by the opaque, pre-determined and confession-based nature of Chinese court proceedings. On the same day of Heywood's alleged extortion email, 12 November, Wang Lijun had arranged 'surveillance and control' of Heywood in Beijing, presumably monitoring his electronic communication and watching his movements. The pretext for Wang's surveillance was that the Englishman was peddling drugs. Nothing is clear about these events, including whether Heywood's email to Bo Guagua triggered Wang's surveillance, or Wang's surveillance uncovered the email, or if the email even exists. According to the prosecution, however, Gu was informed of the email exchange by the family's aide, Zhang Xiaojun, she interpreted it as a physical threat to her son, and it provided her with the motive for Heywood's murder.

Perhaps it was Gu's idea to murder Heywood. Or perhaps, given Gu's general and growing fear about her family's safety, Wang planted the idea in her unstable mind. However it arose, the Chongqing police chief not only condoned the murder but also volunteered to carry it out. 'They would lure him to Chongqing, then use the excuse of his resisting arrest as a drug dealer to shoot him dead on the spot,' says an account of court proceedings by an unofficial observer, Zhao Xiangcha, corroborated by lawyer Li Xiaolin.

Wang, however, backed out of the plan and Gu soldiered on. 'Wang Lijun at first took part in the plot, but later on, perhaps fearing the risk, did not want to continue his participation,' says the unofficial court account. It seems Gu had been drawn into breaking the first rule of survival in the Chinese bureaucracy: that there must be collective ownership and equal vulnerability for all actions at all times. She compounded her error by briefing Wang of her new murder plans on 13 November, just hours before pouring the poison down Heywood's throat. She continued to treat him as a close accomplice after the fact.

After leaving her old friend lying dead or dying in his villa, she phoned Wang, at midnight, and told him the plot had gone to plan. Late on the following morning, Wang drove to the Lucky Holiday Hotel and met her at No. 3 villa, where she gave him a blow-by-blow account. 'I told him in detail about how I met and poisoned Neil on the night of November 13,' said Gu, standing as a witness in the trial of Wang Lijun, according to Xinhua. 'He told me not to be bothered by the case, which would have nothing to do with me in the future. He also told me to erase my memories about the case. I told him I was a bit worried, he told me it would be fine within a week or two.' But as Gu was displaying total trust in Wang, the police chief was secretly recording the entire incriminating conversation. According to Wang's later account to US diplomats, she also told him: 'I killed a spy.' Diplomats familiar with that testimony interpreted Gu's comment as a reference to Heywood seeking information that could be used to privately extort or undermine the family. If Wang was a pawn in a top-level battle over Bo Xilai, Heywood and Gu were pawns in Wang's personal game to save himself. The conspiracies, at all levels, were working better than anyone could have expected.

On 15 November, Chongqing police received a call from the Lucky Holiday Hotel, as expected, saying an Englishman had been found dead in his bed. Wang delegated his deputy, described in court as Gu's 'close friend', to handle the case, along with the head of criminal investigations and head of technical forensics, who were both close protégés of his own. He moved off the case one outsider, whom he could not completely trust. Wang took blood samples from Heywood's heart and stashed them away with other evidence, including the recording of Gu's confession. The team first concluded that Gu was 'highly suspected' of committing a crime, then listed the cause of death as 'alcohol poisoning' and flew to Beijing to convince or intimidate Heywood's wife accordingly. 'They covered up the fact of [Gu Kailai's] presence at the scene by fabricating interview records, hiding material evidence and other measures,' says Xinhua.

On 16 Wednesday, bypassing the usual channels at the Chongqing foreign office, police notified the city's UK consulate that a 41-year-old Englishman had died from drinking too much. Coincidentally, the UK Foreign Office minister Jeremy Browne had arrived and met Bo Xilai that same day, without learning there had been a death. On 18 Friday, Heywood's wife attended a hasty cremation with a junior UK diplomat in Chongqing. Wang phoned Gu and confirmed the job had been done: 'Transformed into a twist of smoke; riding a crane to the west.'

Gu's court testimony that she'd had a 'breakdown' does not seem exaggerated. A photograph taken shortly after the murder shows Gu addressing a meeting of the city's top police officials, including Wang Lijun, at Wang's famous police cafeteria, even though she held no official title of her own. Stranger still is the fact that she's smiling for the camera and wearing an immaculate People's Liberation

Army uniform, fitted to her trim physique, which is decorated with the same major general's two-star insignia that her own father used to wear. 'She said that she was under secret orders from the Ministry of Public Security to effectively protect Comrade Wang Lijun's personal safety in Chongqing,' a source told Reuters, adding that her rambling speech 'was a mess'. It seemed a strange and twisted echo of Mao's wife, Jiang Qing, who had taken to wearing the PLA uniform when Mao empowered her to steer the Cultural Revolution. Mao and Jiang Qing wreaked their destruction on a far greater scale, but murder had been beyond the usual rules of play.

Chinese power is a game of never showing weakness and convincing those who matter that your star is always rising. Bo and Wang had both made their careers by taking this logic to extremes. They both hated taking backward steps and built up an almost mythical aura of invincibility. It may never be known whether Wang betrayed Bo, or if Bo moved first to cut Wang loose, but it is clear that Wang had taken extraordinary precautions to pre-empt such a fate.

Gu and Wang fell out after she called another top-level police banquet, on 14 December. Four of Wang's close staff were immediately placed under investigation, according to the prosecution at Wang's trial, which did not say who had made the order. In early January, a planeload of investigators from the central discipline commission arrived in Chongqing. A week later, Wang's successor as police chief in Tieling city, who had been detained the previous May, was quietly sentenced to twelve years gaol, on corruption charges. The walls were closing in on Wang from all sides, one step removed from Bo Xilai.

The Great Escape

On 28 January, during the Chinese New Year holiday, Wang pulled out his only card. He told Bo of his belief that his wife had arranged the murder of the English businessman and then raised the stakes by suggesting Bo should cooperate with an investigation.[82] Wang thus lit the fuse that could detonate Bo's career and watched for the reaction. The following day they met again. This time Bo was furious. In front of Wang's deputies, Bo delivered the ultimate insult and reprimand for betraying the family, by slapping Wang in the face.

But Wang returned to his office and immediately ordered his personal loyalists in senior police ranks to retrieve the old Gu murder file, blood sample and tapes.

On 2 February, Bo sacked Wang from his police

chief post and placed him in charge of economics, without Bo seeking the usual central government approval. Hours later, Bo's usually slick propaganda team revised its one-line statement, which was sent out on its micro blog, and said Wang would actually be in charge of education, science and the environment. Bo arrested three more of Wang's close associates,[83] including a driver who was rumoured to have died from the experience. Bo's key business operative, Xu Ming, and the former PLA intelligence officer Yu Junshi, tried to broker a reconciliation between China's greatest double-act. They failed. Yu rushed home and stuffed ¥1.2 million in cash into a bag and deposited it in a bank. The pair slipped out of the country together to Australia on Xu Ming's private jet.[84] Wang Lijun, now under the type of suffocating surveillance that he had so often imposed, planned a more elaborate escape.

At dawn on 6 February, after five days with little if any sleep, Wang drove west out of Chongqing. To avoid detection he drove for seven hours on the provincial back roads to Chengdu, around steep river ridges and lush rice paddies, rather than the dual carriage freeway that would have taken half that time. Part way along the journey, at the opening of office hours, Wang had arranged a call to the British consulate in Chongqing to discuss his new portfolio, as a decoy to put his minders off his trail. He made a second call, via the police chief of Sichuan province (who was sacked shortly afterwards), requesting a meeting at the US consulate in Chengdu.

Wang pointed his car to the US consulate because it is controlled by the world's great superpower, it is beyond Bo's formal jurisdiction and it is the only freestanding foreign mission in Southwest China. Unlike the British consulate in Chongqing, which is housed in an ordinary commercial office building, the US consulate is surrounded by gardens and high walls that even Bo Xilai would think twice before invading. Wang's act of near-certain political suicide – which President Hu Jintao would come to call *panguo tuodi* (betraying the country and going over to the enemy) – must have seemed preferable to whatever Bo had waiting for him in Chongqing. Nobody could match Wang's intimate knowledge of Bo's capabilities.

The US consul general happened to be out of town (in Yunnan province with his mobile phone turned off), when China's most famous but now rather flustered mafia-busting cop arrived at the gate at 2.31 p.m. on Monday, 6 February. The two relatively junior US diplomats who greeted him were caught off-guard and didn't invite him into the lead-encased room insulated from Chinese electronic listening devices, which is normally reserved for American citizens. Instead, Wang was ushered into the consulate library. The two diplomats were fluent in Chinese but also called in a US citizen interpreter.

Well aware of Chinese electronic espionage capabilities, and himself an expert in the field, Wang began by bewildering the Americans with a barely coherent thirty-minute spiel about his new education, science and environment portfolio. When it was time to get to the point, according to diplomats close to the unfolding affair, he silently handed over notes on a piece of card that looked as though they had been scribbled in the car. The card contained lurid details of how Gu Kailai had murdered Heywood. Towards the bottom of the card was a more personal note. At this point, the 'iron-blooded police chief' had tears in his eyes. He said he hadn't slept for five days and now feared for his life, after attempting to investigate a crime. Perhaps Wang never said so in as many words, and the US government has repeatedly denied it, but the translator turned to the two diplomats after reading from the card, and said: 'He wants to defect.' [85]

One of the Americans left the room and returned with a tape recorder, which he placed openly on the desk, and over a period of hours they listened to a story about the Bo family's international money laundering, phone tapping and murder – at times self-serving and incomplete – that Hollywood could not have dreamed up. The US diplomats relayed the conversation to the embassy in Beijing, which promptly briefed the British embassy that evening. They recounted Wang's extraordinary claim that Heywood had been murdered by the wife of China's most colourful politician. Some officials who received these reports were deeply invested in the view that the Chinese leadership succession process had become 'institutionalised' and that Chinese leaders would always privilege their collective interests over personal ones. What they were hearing challenged the prevailing global consensus about how China works.

Wang had anticipated that his story would not be an easy sell. He handed over a mobile phone number of a person who was presently in Chongqing, he said, and who could provide evidence to back his claims including a blood sample taken from Heywood's heart. He also gave instructions to open a new email account, to which documents would be sent by the mystery third party. The Americans handed the British the mobile phone number and email account details, with which they could corroborate Heywood's murder.

In Beijing, presumably inside the high vermillion

walls of the old imperial lake palaces of Zhongnanhai, President Hu Jintao promptly received a report that Wang had entered the US mission, relayed from intelligence officers who constantly watch all US diplomatic missions in China. Hu and his nine-member Politburo Standing Committee navigated the treacherous national, factional and personal implications while the outward-facing parts of the Chinese bureaucracy went into meltdown.

The US consulate was soon surrounded by dozens of Chinese armoured vehicles.[86] A gun was poked through the window of a departing car, which contained the family of an American diplomat. US diplomats tried to register their displeasure but could not locate any of their usual contacts in the provincial foreign office. In Beijing, Jon Huntsman's replacement as ambassador, the former US Secretary of Commerce Gary Locke, dialled the mobile phone of his counterpart, Assistant Minister of Foreign Affairs Cui Tiankai, but even he declined to answer. Locke was furious. It was the most fraught diplomatic stand-off in a decade, and US officials could not find anyone of seniority who was game to even pick up the phone before receiving instructions from above. Eventually they reached a lower-level foreign ministry official.

Secure phone lines were lighting up between

Chengdu and the US State Department in Washington. The National Security Council was brought into discussions, although President Barack Obama himself was not interrupted at that stage. When it became clear that Wang's apparent objective of receiving American political asylum was not going to happen for a man accused of systematic torture, he groped for other possible places of refuge to which he could be transported to avoid the clutches of Bo Xilai. He decided on Beijing and the Americans asked if there was someone he wanted to speak to there. He replied that he couldn't really think of anyone.

Chongqing officials finally caught up with the whereabouts of their missing deputy mayor. Mayor Huang Qifan – Wang's rival for Bo's attention – set off in an effort to contain the damage, careering down the highway and arriving in Chengdu late in the evening. He was ushered inside the US consulate while officials from the Chongqing foreign office – known as 'barbarian handlers' in diplomatic circles – loitered awkwardly outside the gates. Huang and Wang were given a meeting room, with no overt recording facilities, as they negotiated Wang's fate. Huang dialled into a high-stakes factional tussle that was taking place over which agency, and which personnel, should take custody of the dangerous witness and of the case. If there are any covert American records of those conversations then they are circulating at a high level of security clearance.

The British, more cautious and conservative than the Americans, delayed before contacting the mobile phone number they had been given. They made belated contact but the delicate communication broke down. By the time Foreign Secretary William Hague was briefed, on 8 February, and indicated that he wanted all avenues pursued, the opportunity had vanished.

Wang exited the consular gates at 11.35 p.m. on 7 February, after thirty-three hours and four minutes under American protection. He left on the condition that he would be handed over to China's Ministry of State Security – the main intelligence and counter-espionage agency – rather than to anyone from Chongqing who might take him back to Bo Xilai.

But there was one last unexpected catch.

Qiu Jin, the vice minister of State Security and Hu Jintao-loyalist who first reported Wang's adventures to top leaders, chartered a government plane to personally escort Wang back to Beijing. But Wang had placed one final condition on his agreeing to leave the US consulate gates. He had claimed to US officials that the Bo family had deliberately brought down a passenger jet from Beijing to Dalian in 2002, killing 112 people, in order to stop an unwelcome messenger from Beijing. It is unlikely Wang had any reliable knowledge of that tragedy – he didn't join the family until 2006 – but nevertheless he demanded a bigger plane, crowded with more people, to stop Bo from doing the same to him.[87]

'Wang insisted on traveling on an ordinary commercial passenger plane, because he was convinced that if it was a special-purpose flight Bo would find a way to blow it up,' a senior Chinese intelligence source said, clearly wishing to explain what might otherwise look like a case of bureaucratic incompetence. 'Wang knew better than anybody what Bo would be prepared to do to prevent him from telling his story in Beijing.'

So this seminal and secretive episode in modern Chinese politics and US–China relations ended with Wang sitting in first class on China Airlines flight 4113, from Chengdu to Beijing, together with a vice minister from an agency so secretive that it doesn't have a phone number, a website or even a nameplate. Their boarding passes were somehow spotted, photographed and immediately pasted over the Chinese-language internet.

The rupturing of China's most famous political double act was a seismic political event, by any measure. It was the first time since the Tiananmen protests of 1989 that a high-ranking Chinese official had chosen to publicly challenge the system rather than fall on his sword. Other than 1989, it was the only Communist Party power struggle that had not played out in total secret. It was the first known attempted high-level defection in at least a quarter of a century, since China's head of US intelligence operations betrayed the country and exposed a veteran Chinese agent inside the CIA. Wang's was probably the highest-level attempted defection since 1971, when Marshal Lin Biao, Chairman Mao's deputy and right-hand man, crashed his Trident aircraft in the grasslands of Mongolia while trying to defect to the Soviet 'revisionists'.

Lin Biao's shock attempted defection was the point at which many Chinese say they lost faith in Mao's revolution. If their esteemed No. 2 leader, and Mao's right-hand man, had no faith in the Great Helmsman and his utopian vision, then who did? Unlike forty years ago, when the Marshal's attempt to abscond was kept secret for almost a year, Wang Lijun was demonstrating his faith in China's great strategic rival – now the United States – right in the midst of China's information revolution. 'The very fact that Wang Lijun would defect to the US consulate suggests to me that [it is] the safest place in China,' said the former US ambassador Jon Huntsman. Chinese netizens circulated photos and well-sourced rumours while censors worked frantically to delete them. Half a billion Chinese internet users had the capability to share and access news outside the Party-state's propaganda apparatus, notwithstanding the best efforts of tens of thousands of internet police. An army of microbloggers provided eyewitness coverage of the stand-off at the US consulate and every publicly visible increment in the story. China's seemingly depoliticised population scoured and translated foreign news reports and jumped the Great Firewall to absorb the mix of fanciful innuendo and genuine inside news being published on dissident Chinese language websites operated overseas. Anybody with access to an internet connection, it seemed, was now talking about Wang Lijun and Bo Xilai.

When Wang Lijun was finally escorted from the US consulate, Bo's usually slick propaganda machine said Wang had merely been 'overworked' and would be taking 'vacation-style therapy'. The vast, and vastly cynical, internet community immediately added the term to its growing list of Communist Party euphemisms and doublespeak. 'Let's continue: consoling-style rape, harmony-style looting, environmental-style murder, scientific-style theft,' said one of 50 000 microblog comments that appeared on the subject that day.

On the same day, Bo Xilai flew south to Kunming

to make an unscheduled public inspection of the headquarters of the 14th Army, which his father had personally founded. At that point, political analysts began to comprehend how Bo Xilai would stop at nothing to achieve his ambitions, even to the point of risking splitting the country. The fact that Bo Xilai had systematically tortured and dispossessed Chongqing officials and entrepreneurs, and had distributed inside deals to his mates, as if it were his personal fiefdom, was never going to be enough to challenge his ascendancy, in a system where brutality and corruption are commonplace. Being responsible for the highest-level attempted defection in forty years, however, was a serious embarrassment. The extent of Bo's political reach and impact became clearer with the prospect of his departure.

From the moment it became clear Bo Xilai was in great trouble, several high-ranking figures stepped forward to endorse or oppose Bo's vision, or otherwise shape the post-Bo world. Bo had spun an astonishingly complex web of patronage, enemies and friends, primarily through his princeling networks. One princeling who counselled against heavy retribution is said to be Chen Yuan. Chen's father had worked alongside Bo Yibo, his bank had helped fund the Chongqing Model and his daughter had dated Bo Guagua. Another was Major General Zhu

Heping, who is the grandson of the commander-in-chief of Mao's Red Army and the public face of China's stealth fighter program. 'Singing red is pretty good,' he told reporters, endorsing Bo's legacy with a smile.[88]

Another supporter was China's fearsome security chief, Zhou Yongkang, who remains a powerful patron of China's oil industry while overseeing a security budget that has now surpassed that of the PLA. While rumours back in March of Zhou's support for Bo extending to an attempted coup seem vastly exaggerated, even his own senior officers concede 'something happened' and that he had fought an internal battle to hand over his security portfolio on the Politburo Standing Committee to Bo Xilai at the November leadership transition. It is likely that Bo would have been made China's new security czar, if not for Wang Lijun's escape to the US embassy.

Members of Bo's inner court, led by businessman Xu Ming, assessed their inside information and became so convinced that he would survive that they flew back to China from Australia to continue sharing in the spoils.

The Fall of Bo, Xi's Rise

Bo Xilai's fate was hanging in the balance in March 2012, when he called his audacious press conference at the National People's Congress. His message, that Communist Party insiders were forming a new capitalist class, was a powerful critique, even if the Party's internal investigators were discovering that his own family was a prime example. After the reporters jammed into the room had exhausted nearly three hours of questions, the Chongqing mayor, Huang Qifan, declared an end to proceedings and moved to leave his chair. But Bo, drawing on his famed aristocratic confidence and family defiance, gestured for the crowd to remain. What he was about to say did not seem addressed to his colleagues, who held his immediate fate in his hands, but to the Chinese public or possibly even a group of leaders who might turn to him for salvation in a time of future crisis. Perhaps he was also playing an inter-generational game, protecting his son's reputation and clearing his path ahead, just as his father had done for him and his grandparents had done for Bo Yibo.

Bo raised his hand and said he had one thing to add. 'I was mentally prepared for the fact that attacking organised crime and expunging evil would affect some people's interests and that there would be different views,' he said. 'And all these people who form criminal cliques have forged broad social ties and they have power to shape opinion. Moreover, for instance, there are many people who have poured filth on Chongqing, including pouring filth on me and my family, even talking about my son studying abroad and driving a red Ferrari – utter nonsense – and makes me feel outraged. Utter nonsense. And not just my son.' Bo said his son's school fees had been entirely paid by scholarships and his wife had given up her successful law practice twenty years ago and closed her firm, to avoid the appearance of a conflict of interest. 'She now basically just stays at home, doing some housework for me,' he said. 'I'm really touched by her sacrifice.' It was a spellbinding performance, even if very little of it was true.

Until that point, Xi Jinping had appeared to stand with Bo in factional solidarity, jointly owing allegiance to former president Jiang Zemin. They had been jointly building their prestige as 'Red Successors' of the communist revolution. Bo Xilai had always held the upper hand in this relationship of convenience. Bo's father had outranked, outlived and out-manoeuvred Xi's father over seven decades of power and purgatory. They had been on opposing sides of some of the Party's great internal rivalries since the 1950s, dating back to a battle between their respective mentors. Bo was seen to be smarter, more charismatic and more courageous, as well as being four years Xi's senior. Bo Xilai was talked about as the true heir of their fathers' revolutionary generation. Few of Bo's peers thought that Xi Jinping would maintain control of him if he made it into the Politburo Standing Committee alongside him. Xi would bring down Bo because he would be 'uncontrollable' in his inner cabinet, said a princeling friend who knew Xi well. 'His behaviour shows he wanted to be number one.' Perhaps it was Bo's utter lack of contrition, humility or subordination that prompted Xi to shift the balance of power in the Politburo Standing Committee. Five days later, on 14 March, Premier Wen Jiabao gave his tenth and final press conference to close the Congress – in which he foreshadowed Bo's political execution.

With theatrical symmetry, after exhausting more

than three hours of questions with eloquent and at times emotional answers, Wen reopened debate on one of the most tumultuous events in the Chinese Communist Party's history and hammered the first nail in the coffin of his great rival. After responding to a gently phrased question about Chongqing he offered an addendum – 'I'd like to say a few words' – that indirectly, but unmistakably, defined Bo as a man who wanted to repudiate China's decades-long effort to reform its economy, open to the world, and allow its citizens to experience modernity. He framed the struggle over Bo's fate and legacy as the culmination of a thirty-year battle for two radically different versions of China. Bringing down Bo was posed as the first step in a battle between China's Maoist past and a more democratic future as personified by Wen's mentor and Xi Jinping's father's close friend, 1980s Communist Party chief Hu Yaobang. Wen's words blew open the facade of party unity that had held since the massacres of Tiananmen Square.

'After the implementation of reform and opening up, the mistakes of the Cultural Revolution and feudalism have not been completely eliminated,' Wen told the 1000 spellbound Chinese and foreign journalists, and tens of millions of citizens watching live on television in their homes. 'Reform has reached a critical stage. Without the success of political reform, economic reforms cannot be carried out. The results that we have achieved may be lost. A historical tragedy like the Cultural Revolution may occur again.'

By linking Bo's imminent demise to the spectre of the Cultural Revolution, Wen Jiabao was not only daring his colleagues to end Bo's career but to use his demise as the impetus to launch the Party's perennially postponed political reforms. He was opening a crack in the vault of Communist Party history: that great black box that conceals the struggles, brutality, partial truths and outright fabrications upon which China has built its staggering economic and social transformation. It was also a repudiation of everything the Bo family was seen to stand for. He was opening the wounds from the schoolyard history, for which princeling Red Guards have never been held to account, even if Bo's purportedly bloodthirsty role has been fabricated. It was a reminder that Bo was in Chongqing echoing the 'red terror' that had killed his own mother.

The following day, 15 March, Bo was sacked from his job as Party boss of Chongqing and placed in detention, as was his wife Gu Kailai, businessman Xu Ming and a host of other close associates. It was a seismic leadership rupture that continues to convulse China's political landscape to an extent not seen since 1989.

In some ways, China continued on in the same manner it had previously. Chinese people were vastly more prosperous than at any time in the nation's history. The Party-state continued to grow stronger, in relation to the rest of the world, while channelling unprecedented resources and authority to its coercive systems to ensure there could be no conceivable challenger to its rule. While the economy was softening, and cracks were opening up in Chinese elite politics, the leaders remained tied together in a delicate factional balance that was buttressed by webs of patronage and corruption. As much as some leaders detested each other, and despite their divergent factional, ideological, personal and bureaucratic interests, any sudden move by an individual leader or group of leaders could result in a counter strike and mutually assured destruction. Policies, ideology and the factional balance remained broadly unchanged. Bo's patron, the master politician Jiang Zemin, wasted little time in jettisoning his maverick political client. Bo, he reportedly said, had 'breached a civilisational bottom line'.

But the Party's facade of unity and its public legitimacy had been battered. Just three days after Bo's dismissal, at 4 a.m. on Sunday, 18 March, the leadership received a sign of deepening cynicism when a black Ferrari Spider 458, reportedly bought for close to $1 million, was travelling so fast that it exploded when it struck the Baofusi bridge, just south of Tsinghua University. The driver, who was killed alongside two scantily clad women in his two-seater car, was immediately presumed to be the son of a Politburo member when censors scrambled to cover up the news.

In the days that followed, the Congress, senior American officials and Wang Lijun's supporters grew impatient at the lack of public action. China had made no public acknowledgement that a murder might have taken place. The Americans had shared almost all of Wang's testimony with the British and intervened to ensure the British did not hand it over to the Chinese. On 24 March, a Shanghai intellectual received a text message about an Englishman being murdered in Chongqing and put it on his microblog. On the evening of 25 March, Reuters broke the news of Heywood's suspicious death. The *Wall Street Journal* immediately added lurid details about poison and Gu Kailai.

The extraordinary story – English man of mystery poisoned by Politburo wife – prompted foreign journalists to dig more deeply into Chinese politics than they had for a generation. The *New York Times* reported that Bo Xilai and Wang Lijun had tapped the phones of top leaders, including Hu Jintao. Bloomberg documented how Bo's elder brother had accumulated US$10 million in shares working on the board of a state-owned financial conglomerate, under an adopted name. The media group discovered that Gu Kailai's siblings, meanwhile, had accumulated assets worth at least US$126 million. Bloomberg moved up the hierarchy to discover that Xi Jinping's siblings held family assets that tallied up to well over 1 billion US dollars, almost all of which was carefully concealed from public view. Even Premier Wen, who led the destruction of his great adversary, ended the year a diminished figure, after the *New York Times* tallied US$2.7 billion of assets that his family members had quietly accumulated. Never before had China's evolving kleptocracy been documented and exposed for all to see.

Coup rumours in late March involving Bo supporter Zhou Yongkang were quickly dismissed, but the steady drumbeat of demands for 'unity' and 'loyalty' to President Hu Jintao in PLA newspapers suggested that the president could not reliably count on either.

On 10 April, the Poltiburo was briefed on preliminary investigations into Gu and Wang. Bo was suspended that evening from his Politburo and Central Committee positions for 'serious' but unspecified violations of Party discipline.

The poster boy for Chinese socialism, who had been lauded by top Chinese leaders and who developed the acclaimed 'Chongqing Model', had been exposed for breathtaking hypocrisy. Patriots and admirers stopped talking about a 'China Model', aware that the tawdry affair may have opened a window onto what had become normal conduct. China's civil society leaders began talking more openly about individual leaders and their policies, correctly judging that the Party was too divided to rein them in. Party Central unplugged the popular Maoist internet platforms that had been supporting Bo's rise, but that was not enough to silence them. The purging of Bo 'might be used by the domestic traitorous forces who collaborate with Western hostile forces to foment social chaos, split China into pieces and bring it to the abyss,' said *Utopia* stalwarts, in a mass email. Bo's absence left a political void, as the Party drifted further towards the end of the post-Mao road map.

Bo Xilai had brilliantly exploited a stretch of weak Communist Party leadership and policy drift that had begun when Hu Jintao ascended to the top job in 2002 and his predecessor, Jiang Zemin, refused to relinquish real power. He played to Hu's ideological predilections, enjoyed the protection of Jiang's patronage umbrella, and leveraged his inherited prestige and connections, and his prodigious political capabilities, to expose the country's accumulating social ailments and turn Chinese politics upside down. His departure, however, left the Party with no convincing narrative to fill the void. The old godfather of the Chongqing mafia, Weng Zhenjie, immediately began courting Bo's temporary replacement, Zhang Dejiang. The whole affair had 'gravely damaged the party and nation's image', Zhang said. Party Central had rid themselves of Bo Xilai but failed to repudiate the ideas of untrammelled state power that he stood for and which enabled his rise to occur.

'It's a sordid tale from start to finish,' said Jon Huntsman, from his peaceful if temporary retirement from American politics. Still, he said, the fact of open political struggle was itself a sign of progress for a population that was 'hungering' for a semblance of transparency.

On 9 August, Gu Kailai stood in the defendant's box at Hefei Intermediate People's Court for the most eagerly awaited court case since that of Chairman Mao's wife, Jiang Qing, thirty-two years before. The partial information that leaked out to the public left many observers baffled by her motive for murdering Heywood and perplexed by gaping holes in the forensic evidentiary trail. Public doubts about the proceedings ran so deep that the phrase 'body double' was censored on the Chinese internet, after netizens questioned whether the frumpy woman shown in court on the television news was really the glamorous lady who had swept Bo Xilai away from his first wife. 'It's highly likely that an impostor Gu replaced the real Gu; this is all a well-planned scheme,' said Han Deqiang, a co-founder of *Utopia*. 'It's a conspiracy against Bo Xilai.'

China's Maoists and liberals were momentarily united in believing that Gu's trial was a badly scripted sham. 'Lies have to be used to cover up lies, leading to an impossible situation where the story doesn't hold together and it becomes a satire of justice,' wrote He Weifang, professor of law at Peking University, who had been at the forefront of a civil society backlash against Bo Xilai's abuse of law in Chongqing. The proceedings had all the hallmarks of justice by political committee and wound up satisfying no one. The Party, it seemed, was so out of sorts it had failed to put on a convincing show trial.

Beyond the Bo family, the trial revealed an astonishing willingness on the part of top government officials to facilitate a cold, calculated and apparently pointless murder. 'The conduct, completion and attempted cover-up of murder was done directly through the exercise of public power,' wrote Chen Youxi, who had boldly represented the lawyer Li Zhuang in Chongqing. 'Such behaviour only happened in the age of feudal fiefdoms and vassal states.' The Gu case offered 'a starting point to examine recent events that could shape China's history,' wrote Hu Shuli, the editor of the magazine *Caixin*, who had been the first to publish Chen's explosive Cultural Revolution essay one year before.

At the Heywood murder trial, Zhang Xiaojun, the family retainer, earnestly told the court he wanted to say 'sorry' to the relatives of the victim, before he was sentenced to nine year's gaol. 'I really know that I did wrong.' Gu, in contrast, talked not of the morality of her conduct but of the harm she had done to the image of the Party-state: 'The case has produced great losses to the party and the country.' Ominously, for Bo Xilai, both she and Wang Lijun in his separate trial were given lenient treatment in light of evidence they had given about 'the serious crimes of others'. Gu, who said she had acted to protect Bo Guagua, was given a suspended death sentence, which is expected to be commuted to a prison term of perhaps a dozen years. Wang Lijun was sentenced to fifteen years. Heywood himself remained a mystery, after playing his tragic walk-on role in the drama.

As if the Party's public relations challenges could

get any worse, after simmering for five months without official clarification, in September the story of the black Ferrari landed for the first time on the front page of the *South China Morning Post*, just weeks before what was looming as the most precarious Communist Party leadership transition since 1989. It turned out that China's cynical public had been too hasty in presuming that it was the son of the nation's No. 4 leader, Jia Qinglin, who had been driving that sleek overcrowded machine. It turned out that the name 'Jia' had been a police cover-up, which Jia Qinglin had taken as a factional frame-up, initiated by Hu Jintao's most trusted and powerbroker, Ling Jihua. President Hu's predecessor and nemesis, Jiang Zemin, saved up his information that the deceased driver was actually Ling's son, not Jia's, and detonated it to maximum effect. Ling was removed from his position in charge of the General Office. Hu Jintao – who had played a role in Bo's spectacular unravelling – began to look a tragic figure.

The spotlight turned to the anointed king among the princelings, Xi Jinping, when he disappeared for an entire fortnight without any explanation, just when he was supposed to be preparing to take the reins of the world's rising super power. The expected announcement of a date for the 18th Party Congress failed to materialise.

Xi's flattery of Bo in 2010, which had taken up the whole front page of the *Chongqing Daily* and twenty minutes on the evening television news, had long since been expunged from the mainland Chinese internet. Xi's friends claimed he never uttered the words that the state-owned papers and television voiceover attributed to him. They were confident that Xi would, in the final judgment, stand by the memory of his father, who had stood on the opposing side to Bo's father in the first great clash of the People's Republic, the purge of Gao Gang in 1954, and again in the 1987 purge of Hu Yaobang, which still divides liberals and conservatives in the Party today.

As the months stretched on without any official word, however, fears grew that the purge of Bo Xilai was not going to plan. There were credible reports that Bo was following his family's tradition by refusing to submit to a confession. His beloved son, Bo Guagua, was overseas and therefore could not be easily used as leverage. Unless a political stake was thrust through Bo's heart, perhaps he could return as a saviour-figure?

In the logic of Communist Party politics, a fulsome purge can provide the Party with the internal enemy it requires to rally itself against. Destroying Bo would give Xi a weapon with which he could taint Bo's associates and accelerate the consolidation of his power. Liberals desperately hoped that a comprehensive purge would also propel the Party to resume its long-stalled political reforms – charting the future by defining an unwanted past. Some even hoped for a major public trial, like that of Mao's wife, Jiang Qing, which had marked the end of the Mao era, the commitment to reforms and the ascendancy of Deng Xiaoping.

On 29 September, after five months without mentioning Bo's name, Xinhua finally reported that the Politburo had reached agreement on his fate. He had taken massive bribes, personally and through his family, and had improper sexual relations with multiple women. He even shared some responsibility for the murder case, the Politburo charged, apparently referring to allegations that he obstructed the investigation into Gu. He was also suspected of unnamed other crimes. The severity of the accusations, and especially the dangerously open-ended 'other crimes' that they were said to extend back all the way to his time in Dalian, surprised almost all observers. The divided Politburo, after months of negotiations, had empowered the incoming Xi administration to obliterate Bo's reputation.

—

Before his universe imploded, Bo Guagua had aspired to 'serve the people' and believed that the dream of the New China that his grandparents had created remained very much alive. His parents and grandparents had all treated him as the prodigal son. To his friends, Bo Guagua had passionately defended the virtues of the Communist Party, despite his family's brutal battles with it and his own expensive tastes. 'I am very influenced by my father,' he said, in a 2009 interview now expunged from the internet. 'You have to work harder than everyone else and be tougher than everyone else if you want to do get things done.' Bo Guagua is not yet ready to close the book on his family's glorious revolutionary history, passed down from each of his four grandparents and proudly displayed on his father's office walls. Both of his grandfathers had emerged more powerful than ever after spending years in gaol. His parents had endured unfathomable hardships and there was no reason to think they would not do so again.

In the dying days of the Cultural Revolution, a capable, ambitious and deeply disoriented Bo Xilai would sit and stare at photographs of himself, believing that an image of the face can reveal the character within. His mother had been dead eight years and he hadn't seen his father since he was placed in purgatory at the same time. Twenty-five-year-old Bo Xilai had spent most of that time in a prison camp, where he and other princeling children were expected to denounce their fathers. He courted the woman who would become his first wife by composing a poem that honoured the blood spilt by the martyrs of his father's generation, while distancing his own disgraced parents. 'Forget the family for the sake of nation,' he wrote, in a poem that broadly mirrors Chairman Mao's most famous verse, in which Mao made plain his lofty ambitions and self-regard.[89] Bo asked his wife-to-be to join him as he set forth with great resolve to shoulder 'the burning expectations' of the people.[90] With Mao approaching his death bed at the time, he also posed the question he has sought to answer since the onset of the Cultural Revolution: 'I ask China's children, who will be the successors?'[91] Bo Xilai's first wife has treasured that poem, together with letters and photographs from the time. The face in some of those portraits is strikingly similar to that of Bo's son today.

Bo Guagua, who turns twenty-five in December 2012, watched his father's gradual purge and his mother's murder conviction from the US, where he has graduated from Harvard and is said to be preparing to enter law school. He has cooperated with investigators and worked assiduously to protect his own reputation. He liaised and negotiated with Western journalists, occasionally giving statements to dispel damaging misconceptions. 'I have never driven a Ferrari,' he wrote in the *Harvard Crimson*.

Bo Guagua spoke out as soon as the devastating official accusations were made against his father. 'Although the policies my father enacted are open to debate, the father I know is upright in his beliefs and devoted to duty,' he said on his Tumblr social media account. 'Personally, it is hard for me to believe the allegations that were announced against my father, because they contradict everything I have come to know about him throughout my life.' He was defending his father's honour, and also his own.

Bo Guagua has lived half his life as an exiled prince-in-waiting, under the burden of his family's suffocating love and towering expectations, and yet has managed to prove himself in a foreign language against the best and brightest in the world. His father would forgive him for saying what he had to say to save himself and rebuild the family name, just as Bo Yibo had forgiven Bo Xilai for his denunciation sessions at Camp 789. On 2 October, four days after Bo Xilai was officially condemned, Bo Guagua had an email exchange with an acquaintance in which he confessed to being guilty of frivolity, at times, and stressed that he had never abused his own background for personal gain. But his mind was set firmly on the future. 'I now have the chance to live my own life and make my own choices,' he said.

ACKNOWLEDGEMENTS

I am in the debt of many who have assisted in the never-ending battle to understand the workings of modern China. Special thanks are due to the friendship and sage advice of Warren Sun, the master historian of elite Chinese politics; Chris Buckley, doyen of the Beijing foreign press corps; and Don Xia, who patiently explained to me back in 2009 that Chongqing was the key to China's future. My employers at Fairfax have my gratitude for grasping the importance of the China story and giving me rare licence to explore the entrails of politics and policy. My colleague, Sanghee Liu, has been a model of good, calm judgment and integrity. My deepest gratitude goes to my incomparable wife, Tara.

NOTES

1   He Guoqian was previously Party Secretary of Chongqing.

2   See appendices to: http://books.google.com/books/about/
    Politics_at_Mao_s_Court.html?id=kAGOykXxG-4C

3   Bo Yibo and Xi Zhongxun held rival economic portfolios in the
    1950s and the major purge of the People's Republic pitted their
    respective patrons against each other.

4   Chairman Mao had chosen his successor, Hua Guofeng,
    while Deng Xiaoping and his comrades-in-arms including
    Bo Yibo had anointed Hu Yaobang, Zhao Ziyang, Jiang Zemin
    and Hu Jintao.

5   www.nytimes.com/2012/10/07/world/asia/excerpts-of-bo-xilais-
    love-letter-to-his-first-wife-li-danyu.html

6   Although even this detail is disputed by some of Bo's ideological
    and personal supporters.

7   Contributing to rumours that she was in fact born in 1963, the
    Year of the Rabbit, five years after the date attributed by Xinhua.

8   www.nytimes.com/2012/05/01/world/asia/in-china-details-in-
    bo-guagua-episode-challenged.html

9   Liu Huixuan, who later wrote a novel about the Cultural
    Revolution, *When the Sun Sets,* under the pseudonym Li Ping.

10 Interviews with classmates.

11 Interviews with Bo's classmates, including class monitor Fu Yang.

12 Interview with Wang Zu'e, No. 4 alumni.

13 Memoir of Liu Dong in online Cultural Revolution magazine
    Remembrance, www.xujuneberlein.com/rem52.html

14 Yin Hongbia www.xujuneberlein.com/rem52.html#F

15 Kuai Daifu was the Red Guard leader. Quoted in:
    http://lup.lub.lu.se/luur/download?func=downloadFile&
    recordOId=534328&fileOId=625453

16 Premier Zhou Enlai had approved his sick leave.

17 Relating to a statement he was instructed by his superiors
    to sign in order to get out of a Kuomintang gaol.

18 http://washeng.net/HuaShan/BBS/shishi/gbcurrent/199862.shtml

19 http://books.google.com/books/about/China_s_Cultural_
    Revolution_1966_1969.html?id=Qvo5sUPuaKEC

20 Bo Yibo's daughter Bo Xiaoying: http://v.ifeng.com/his/201102/
    b415f0d3-e7fd-481c-9cd2-29be6f9e3502.shtml

21 'Bo Yibo has an attitude problem' in Michael Schoenhals, ed,
    The Cultural Revolution 1966–1969: Not a Dinner Party,
    p.122.

22 Memoir of Duan Ruoshi in *Remembrance*, www.xujuneberlein.
    com/rem72.html#CC

23 Memoir of Duan Ruoshi in *Remembrance*, www.xujuneberlein.
    com/rem72.html#CC

24 http://blog.sina.com.cn/s/blog_4c0141c10102eofo.html ; http://
    www.epochtimes.com/gb/12/2/19/n3517000.htm%E8%96%84
    %E7%86%99%E6%9D%A5%E5%85%B6%E4%BA%BA%
    EF%BC%88%E4%B8%80%EF%BC%89-%E6%96%87%E9
    %9D%A9%E2%80%9C%E8%81%94%E5%8A%A8%E2%
    80%9D%E6%AC%A0%E8%A1%80%E5%80%BA-

25 http://blog.sina.com.cn/s/blog_4c0141c10102eofo.html

26 Interview with Fu Yang, August 2012.

27 Interview, June 2012.

28 Interviews with Party historians.

29 See *The Chronicles of Hu Yaobang Thought*, edited by
    Li Shengping.

30 Hu Yaobang conversation with Australian ambassador
    to China, Ross Garnaut (my father) in 1986.

31 www.smh.com.au/world/a-remarkable-comeback-20100528-wlga.html

32 Deng said 'He who does not reform can stand down,' in comments not recorded in the *Selected Works of Deng Xiaoping*. Bo relayed his response to a close associate interviewed by Monash University historian Warren Sun.

33 Bo Yibo wrote a letter to this effect to Central Committee members in 2002, according to Zhang Musheng, a princeling intellectual and associate of Bo Xilai, Interview, January 2012.

34 Interview with Lloyd Donaldson, former manager of the Dalian Swissotel, who catered for Jiang at the seaside villa.

35 www.faluninfo.net/article/38/

36 http://english.peopledaily.com.cn/200704/12/eng20070412_365883.html

37 www.thechinastory.org/yearbooks/yearbook-2012/chapter-2-symbolic-cities-and-the-cake-debate/

38 http://en.wikipedia.org/wiki/CowParade

39 http://www.bbc.co.uk/news/world-asia-china-17390723

40 Interviews with business associates of Xu Ming.

41 Yu Junshi.

42 A businessman who dealt with Xu Ming believes the introduction involved Bo's wife Gu Kailai and a second figure in Tieling, the comedian and otherwise colourful businessman Zhao Benshan. Another businessman, Jiang Mingyu, says he was also introduced to Wang Lijun by Xuming and Zhao Benshan.

43 Barry Naughton, *The Chinese Economy*, MIT Press, 2007, p. 186; cf official figure of 28.2 million.

44 http://www.china.org.cn/english/MATERIAL/76473.htm

45 Interview with businessman who had dealings with Xu Ming at the time.

46 Interview with businessman who had dealings with Xu Ming and Wen Ruchun.

47 http://ajw.asahi.com/article/special/bo_xilai/AJ201207270011g

48 Li Xuefeng became Beijing Party Secretary and head of the military region following the 1966 purge of Peng Zhen, father of Bo's classmate Fu Yang.

49 www.nytimes.com/2012/10/07/world/asia/bo-xilais-former-wife-reveals-paranoid-side-of-a-once-powerful-chinese-family.html?pagewanted=all&_r=0

50 http://online.wsj.com/article/SB10001424052702303299604577327472813686432.html

51 *Chengdu Evening News*, May 21, 2009, courtesy of Lucy Hornby at Reuters.

52 http://article.netor.com/article/memtext_13412.html

53 'Iron Lady' Wu Yi. Business sources say Premier Wen Jiabao's relationship with Bo had not yet deteriorated at that time.

54 http://www.thechinastory.org/yearbooks/yearbook-2012/chapter-2-symbolic-cities-and-the-cake-debate/

54 http://online.wsj.com/article/SB10001424052702303459004577359972617862832.html

56 Information from Tim Murray, J Capital Research.

57 Interview with Chris Buckley, Reuters.

58 www.theage.com.au/world/bo-paints-the-town-red-invokes-mao-and-jails-gangsters-20110806-1igi7.html

59 Interview with Wang Boming, March 2012.

60 www.smh.com.au/business/show-them-the-money-old-china-20110325-1ca3f.html

61 www.smh.com.au/business/show-them-the-money-old-china-20110325-1ca3f.html#ixzz25zGgYix3

62 Interviews with Yang Fang and with a princeling Red Guard leader who was also at the scene.

63 Lawyer Zhu Mingyong: http://chinalawandpolicy.com/tag/zhu-mingyong/

64 www.smh.com.au/world/children-of-the-revolution-20100212-nxjh.html#ixzz29Us64Itw

65 Although the businessman Xu Ming had bridged some of the distance between Wen and Bo around the beginning of last decade.

66 Interview, February 2011

67 Interview, March 2012.

68 http://cmp.hku.hk/2012/02/10/18952/

69 www.nytimes.com/2012/04/26/world/asia/bo-xilai-said-to-have-spied-on-top-china-officials.html?pagewanted=all

70 Yuan Weiliang, whose body was found in Shenyang's Muddy River.

71 Courtesy of Lucy Hornby, Reuters, who retrieved the story.

72 Xinhua account of Wang's trial: http://news.xinhuanet.com/english/indepth/2012-09/19/c_131861108.htm

73 http://news.xinhuanet.com/english/indepth/2012-09/19/c_131861108_3.htm

74 http://news.xinhuanet.com/english/indepth/2012-09/19/c_131861108.htm

75 www.smh.com.au/business/the-princelings-20101001-16l3l.html

76 www.bloomberg.com/news/2012-04-26/son-of-bo-xilai-says-father-s-ouster-destroyed-my-life-.html

77 www.nytimes.com/2012/10/07/world/asia/bo-xilais-former-wife-reveals-paranoid-side-of-a-once-powerful-chinese-family.html?pagewanted=all&_r=0

78 Tom Reed, *The Times*.

79 http://news.xinhuanet.com/english/china/2012-08/11/c_131776969.htm

80 As well as the Xinhua account, materials have been drawn from an account by an unofficial court observer, Zhao Xiangcha, translated by Don Clarke. http://lawprofessors.typepad.com/china_law_prof_blog/2012/08/unofficial-report-of-proceedings-in-the-gu-kailai-trial.html, and also interviews with Li Xiaolin, the lawyer for the family of co-accused Zhang Xiaojun: www.washingtonpost.com/world/gu-kailai-wife-of-bo-xilai-does-not-contest-murder-charge-at-closed-trial-in-china/2012/08/09/24153ebc-e206-11e1-ae7f-d2a13e249eb2_story_1.html

81 Wang Lijun trial: http://news.xinhuanet.com/english/indepth/2012-09/19/c_131861108.htm

82 According to Wang's subsequent account to US diplomats and also the Xinhua court account of his trial.

83 Xinhua report of Wang's trial.

84 *New York Times*.

85 This account from inside the consulate rests on interviews with UK, US and Australian officials briefed on the proceedings, as well as Chinese intelligence officials.

86 Some senior officials believe the armed vehicles included some that were sent without central authorisation across provincial lines by Bo Xilai. Others say there is no evidence. The Chongqing mayor, Huang Qifan, denied the story on Pheonix television.

87 Dalian journalist Jiang Weiping makes a similar claim, saying the plane was brought down in order to stop an unwelcome messenger from the new Hu Jintao administration. Jiang says he heard the theory from the husband of the allegedly targeted state security official who was on board that plane, with whom Jiang shared a prison cell.

88 http://news.sohu.com/20120304/n336648080.shtml

89 www.marxists.org/reference/archive/mao/selected-works/poems/poems18.htm

90 'Blood a crimson spring. Placing nation before family...'. See http://bbs.aboluowang.com/viewthread.php?tid=65610

91 www.nytimes.com/interactive/2012/10/07/world/asia/07wife-excerpts.html?ref=asia

PENGUIN
SPECIALS

THE DESERTED NEWSROOM

Gideon Haigh

In the last decade, customary news media have crumbled before the effects of the internet on advertising, circulation and viewership. In the next decade, they will be supplemented, if not supplanted, by new news media. In this insightful, informative and candid survey of possible futures, veteran journalist Gideon Haigh considers the options for his industry and his craft. Who wins? Who loses? What are the implications for practitioners, professionals, politicians and the public?

Gideon Haigh has been a journalist for almost thirty years, contributed to more than a hundred newspapers and magazines, written twenty-six books and edited seven others.

GOVERNOR BLIGH AND THE SHORT MAN

A NOVELLA

Peter Cochrane

Seventeen years after the mutiny on the *Bounty*, Governor-elect William Bligh sets sail for New South Wales accompanied by his daughter Mary. A cultured young Englishwoman, Mary is a complete novice at sea. She is entirely unprepared for life on the convoy that sets sail from Portsmouth in 1806: for the unfamiliar rituals, the great emptiness of the ocean, the terrifying storms, the bedazzling natural wonders. Most troubling of all is the bizarre quarrel between her father and the captain of the convoy, Joseph Short, a man whose sensitivities are almost a match for William's and whose temper brings the voyagers to the brink of catastrophe.

Peter Cochrane is an award-winning historian whose accolades include the inaugural Prime Minister's Prize for Australian History. Among his previous books are *Colonial Ambition* and *Australians at War*, the companion volume to the ABC TV series.

PENGUIN
SPECIALS

DYING FOR A CHAT

THE COMMUNICATION BREAKDOWN BETWEEN DOCTORS AND PATIENTS

Ranjana Srivastava

Ranjana Srivastava contends that the best medicine begins with a good chat, to guide the decision-making of both doctors and patients. Increasingly, people are unable to properly comprehend the complex treatment choices on offer, or are self-diagnosing and demanding unnecessary or risky procedures. Doctors, in turn, feel unable to turn down the requests of patients and their families. Narrow specialisation also means no-one is discussing the overall picture of a patient's health. Srivastava warns that people are suffering – even dying – as a result, and the medical profession should be taking responsibility. In a frank and clear-eyed assessment of an unacknowledged crisis, she makes an impassioned case for healthcare training to incorporate effective communication skills.

Dr Ranjana Srivastava is the author of *Tell Me the Truth* and has been widely published in medical journals. She was the winner of the 2012 MJA, MDA National, Nossal Global Health Prize, and practises oncology in Melbourne's public hospital system.